THE
PLACE

THE PLACE
HaMakom

IAN HEARD

WIPF & STOCK · Eugene, Oregon

Wipf and Stock Publishers
199 W 8th Ave, Suite 3
Eugene, OR 97401

The Place
Ha Makom Where Jerusalem's Temples Stood
By Heard, Ian
Copyright©2015 by Heard, Ian
ISBN 13: 978-1-5326-3042-2
Publication date 4/5/2017
Previously published by Tate Publishing & Enterprises, LLC, 2015

Acknowledgements

Whilst I can claim to be the author of this book, it represents, as do all books, the fusion and product of a myriad influences; of mentors too many to list, and heroes near and far. I appreciate them all.

There is, however, a generous and warm-hearted Jew who lives in Sydney with whom I became acquainted during my research. Kevin Bermeister is an entrepreneur with a zeal for Jerusalem, both ancient and future, that has led him to initiate Jerusalem 5800 (www.jerusalem5800.com), a master plan for the Jerusalem metropolitan area. I am indebted to Kevin for his gracious input, his patient assistance with Hebrew words and grammar—and his sense of humor!

My thanks also go to my brother, Rod Heard, a gifted musician and graphic designer (who will, of course, compose the music to go with the film of the book!) who assisted with the cover design. The artwork on the cover, *Palace of King David,* is by permission from the artist Balage Balogh of Archeaology Illustrated, whose work brings history to life. The picture gives his impression of not only King David's Palace (viewed from the north), but also of the walled structure surrounding the Gihon Spring at left, on the hillside into the Kidron Valley.

—Ian Heard
Sydney
June 2015

Contents

Preface 9
1. Babylon Man: Hollowness and Vanity 13
2. The Hint Out of Nowhere 37
3. Yerushalem Man:
   Substance and Multiplication 47
4. A Surprise for Yaakov at the Place 59
5. Seek the Place! 73
6. Yeshua, Bayth-El, and Ay 79
7. Tzion Is Ours! 91
8. The Place Changes Hands 95
9. The Tent at Ghikhon 105
10. Darkness 109
11. I Am Yosiayuh 121
12. Homeward Bound! 125
13. I Am Zekharayah 133
14. Ground Zero 137
15. I Am Petros 141
16. The Place Gets a Makeover! 147

Appendix 1 161

Preface

Religions all lay claim to sacred places usually believed to be where heaven, or the spiritual realm, touches earth and mankind's material realm—Delphi in Ancient Greece, Cusco in Peru, Easter Island, Mecca in Saudi Arabia, and many others. Connection or reconnection to Origin or Source is a thirst that lies deep within the heart of man. It is to be expected that people everywhere, in "groping after God,"[1] to use the apostle Paul's thought, would seek to invest meaning and power in locations. But they cannot all be the thirst quencher.

As natural thirst implies the existence of water, this thirst also implies a single, genuine corresponding answer. In his search, mankind has made many attempts to manufacture an answer. One early attempt to establish reconnection was Bavel, but Bavel arose from the heart and mind of man and from a deception and a lie. The genuine answer was a

---

1. Acts 17:27.

place to which Creator would lead them if they would but allow Him.

Israel's great prophet Ezekiel called Jerusalem the navel of the world (see Ezek. 38:12, where the Hebrew phrase means just that) and in Ezekiel 5:5, God says, "I have set her in the midst [or center] of the nations." And Jerusalem was different. It was everything that Bavel was not, because it was God's idea. In the author's view, that place, *the place*, was actually located where the story of man had begun and, indeed, where it will be finalized. That original location remained the center of God's master plan to redeem fallen mankind and creation to something beyond its original glory, for that is the nature of *His* redeeming grace!

At *the place* (in anglicized Hebrew, *ha makom*), a stream flowed from a spring. Gihon has been vital to the life of Jerusalem for a long time. It is an image and echo of the life-giving, redemptive stream that ever flows from God's presence. In the author's view, Jerusalem's temples were never on what has become known as the Temple Mount but were constructed above the Gihon Spring, a view for which there is a growing body of scholarly support,[2] which

---

2. See, for example, *The Temples That Jerusalem Forgot* by Ernest L. Martin and *Misunderstandings about Jerusalem's Temple Mount* and other essays by Professor Emeritus George Wesley Buchanan.

THE PLACE

coincidentally and significantly makes the Jewish desire to rebuild the temple a realistic possibility!

This is the story of that center, the authentic navel of the earth—the place—the locus around which God built His redeeming plan for us, for you. The place must never assume more importance than its role in the plan. Yet because *He* chose it for a purpose, it has importance and should point us to Him and to that grand and beautiful purpose for which it was chosen.

Some of the characters the reader will recognize as historic, from the pages of your Bible; some are invented and placed within the biblical context of the great epochs. Consider!

(Note: It will assist readers to understand a few Hebrew word forms, viz., ha makom translates as 'the place', ha being the definite article; ba makom includes the definite article and translates as 'to (or in) the place' and u makom also includes the definite article and translates as 'and the place'.)

1

Babylon Man: Hollowness and Vanity

Hollowness

The plain country enjoyed four distinct seasons. Grazing and cropping possibilities were encouraging, and the abundance of new building materials seemed to make a long-dreamed-of prospect possible. For within everyone's deep place (for one, near obsession; for another, a vague yearning) resided a desire to recapture *something*. A vestige, sensed as once having been held and occupied but now existing as a phantom only or a tantalizing hint. Something that danced, wraith-like, just outside conscious knowing, as a mirage or a distant nebula is more noticed by peripheral vision than direct gaze, a thing defying clear definition and yet calling, at times softly or at other times stridently, for resolution.

For some time following the great deluge, they had journeyed gradually westward, seeking room and arable land and opportunity as their numbers grew; but as both geographical and generational distance from Father Noe increased, so too did forgetfulness about what the great man of faith and faithfulness had taught. The lessons grew dim and seemed less relevant, and besides, with the tedium of food and shelter and livelihood, it was just easier to let them fade away. But the forgetting left a strange hollowness, which they failed to attribute to that which they had neglected.

Yachim spoke, and his strong, leathery features characterized the resolve in his voice. "See this country?" he enthused to his son and his wife, but the words rippled quickly through the greater throng, for Yachim (the one who establishes) was well respected and honored among the people. "Here we can, at last, make a real life for ourselves. I really feel the promise of something here—the answer for the longings of which we've all spoken."

Most of those near him nodded agreement, as much from habit as from conviction, and took another look, perhaps hoping to see what Yachim saw.

But the promise in Yachim's voice was assuring and strong: "We'll never be scattered or feel afraid or alone again."

They stood on a slight prominence, and a warm zephyr whispered past them, carrying hinted scents of pine and fresh field grasses warmed by spring sunshine. No question,

THE PLACE

the vista was beautifully alluring and redolent with promise, a scene to lift optimism and create confidence, especially if you were someone of Yachim's cup-half-full disposition. Two great rivers watered this land. Some had already started to call one Tiigra, for it flowed very boldly and swiftly, and the other was becoming known as Ufratu because it seemed so productive.

Under her breath, her face half-turned from him and her mouth hidden from his view by tangled black tresses, his one wife ventured. "Yachim, you're always so full of your grand schemes and ideas, like wanting another son! So now we have eight mouths to feed and still no brother for our only son and barely enough food for three! When will we ever find this thing...this place you dream of? When will we feel we're not always trying to escape something...or find something? Even this land you insisted on bringing us to just keeps on stretching away in unfulfilled promise of vain horizons!" Yachim's attractive wife too was capable of succinct expression. She was much more a glass-half-empty person, or what she called a realist. She added, "Where does this, er, this hollowness end?" It trailed away in a sigh.

"You'll see! You'll see!" Yachim's tone and the set of his bearded chin were now defiant, his robust nose glistening where the late sun caught his oily skin. "Here we'll get established. We'll become what we desire. We'll build things. We'll know who we are. There's the answer to your... what did you call it? Hollowness?" And then in sweeping rhetoric, which began to move beyond a simple desire to build for shelter, comfort, and safety, he said, "Here we can be established and make ourselves all we are intended to be—a people of renown. We'll work together to become masters of our destiny, make a name for ourselves. What's going to stop us?"

Yachim's wife toyed with her hair and used it to brush a salty trickle from her cheek until a needy child's cry called her back to necessity.

And so tents were pitched in the delightful plain. Perhaps soon the within-sense of disquiet, at times foreboding, would be a thing of the past?

The hollowness could also be described as a lessness, a sense of something disquietingly absent and making its absence felt; a vacancy that teased, most generally manifesting itself as a drab-gray, only-just-there background shadow of doubt behind every duty and event; behind life itself, albeit sometimes temporarily subsumed by beauties or food and wine and pleasures and passions of love and laughter. But the hollowness, the lessness, didn't always whisper, for there were occasions when it clamored for attention; but loud or soft, it always suggested a quest for repleteness.

Where did certainty and connectedness live? For instance, about the "I am" sense within each one and arising from that, the "Why am I?" and questions of value and direction and reasons for things, about place and significance in whatever the scheme was, and, indeed, if there was any

THE PLACE

scheme. And about peacefulness and a sense of arrival at a nonhollowness that might perchance supplant the dread-bringing feelings of vulnerability that could easily engulf as life was observed and experienced. There was a yearning for a settled assurance of connectedness, of belonging, of place within the larger entirety. Within (and sometimes enveloping) was this shadow awareness of transience, impermanence, or disconnectedness from continuity and from purpose or meaning.

Sometimes it was not too strong to say it was a sense of banishment, of having been consigned to an existence falling short of the tease that remained alive within. At times, the tease cruelly ruled. Did it point to anything actually possible, albeit by some means as yet undiscovered, or was it bound forever to remain a hollow promise? Was there actually some eventual and life-giving connection that the hollowness and the lessness seemed to imply? After all, did not thirst on a hot day similarly imply, even presuppose, the existence of that soft, clear answering water that Creator had supplied? Did not bread answer and satisfy the lessness experienced in the stomach? Yes, these were the phantoms that often defined and characterized life, at least for Yachim's wife and many others.

Yachim was confident that the answer to all these was now near at hand! And Yachim was a persuasive and clever man. He was the ubersexual male of his day—sensitive, given to causes, persuasive, and self-confident. At least that's how he liked to come across, and he thought he did.

For those more reflective and less self-assured than Yachim, there was another, a second kind of yearning too. Just beyond fingertips was a sought-for comfort that life actually signified something other than an endless struggle against a cosmos that knew only how to respond with defiance and taunts. Vanity seemed somehow programmed into the scheme, with its tendency to work more against rather than for fruitfulness and reciprocity. Only by the sweat of their brow could the system grudgingly be persuaded into a measure of cooperation. All that they'd experienced up 'til now pointed to the same lessness rather than to substance, permanence, or eternity as they wrested from uncooperative and hostile ground a measure of sustenance.

They longed for a better principle that they sensed should be there somewhere. Any triumph achieved was short-lived and remained only while maintained against onslaughts of decay, weeds, corrosion, insects, disease, or conquest by others. Was this all there was?

Any effort to signify something required as great an effort to preserve as it did to establish. Diminishing returns dictated greater expenditures of time and effort. Utility always succumbed eventually to futility. Significance seemed all but lost to the thrall of decay.

THE PLACE

Then, as alluded to before, there was the hovering sense of vulnerability to the unseen and unknown. What was the dread that had squatted in the depth of hearts, casting its gray and silent pall over thinking, actions, and days? A shadowy pall, neither visible nor tangible yet often crippling. This nemesis, born partially from catastrophe witnessed in earthquake, eruption, flood, fire, famine and disease (and powerlessness against such events) and partly from fear of other as yet unwitnessed possibilities, but it was more than that too. A far-in sense of insecurity that tyrannized, creating an accustomed, underlying anxiety that was hard to ignore—and harder to escape. There it was, like a pebble in a sandal, a constant though just perceptible aggravation. It nagged because the reality and inevitability of death brought questions without answers because disease, sickness, and impairment created a *why* in the heart, for which every contrived answer seemed only to serve to write the *WHY* in yet larger letters.

And so desire to be reconnected, to know significance, to instead enjoy a sense of calm shalom even amid adversity—these described the hollowness that drove man in the days of which I write.

Hollow Man moved westward after the Deluge and found the plain; the conditions, the possibilities, it seemed, for which he had been searching. Here, perhaps, he could become Replete Man. That was the hope. The plain, to Yachim at least, seemed full of bright expectation—

expectation of mastery over the vagaries which, until now, had mastered them. Here could be created a sense of place and connectedness, the scattering and sense of homelessness known since the great deluge would be over, and here would be established meaning and significance; a sense of "arrival" would minister its balm. And here—could it be possible?—would be reconnection with whatever it was that had been lost. The hollowness and the lessness would be diminishing memories.

Something remarkable occurred one day that helped to turn the remaining sceptics among them to true believers.

Technology to the Rescue?

Yachim's brother Riphath was a curious and inventive man. He fashioned new iron spearheads and experimented with fire, wood, and varieties of stone. He and a son had one day, after fresh rainfall, dammed with mud a small tributary that flowed into a creek where they looked for fish. Days later when they returned that way, the water had drained and evaporated, and under several days of hot sun, the mud had congealed to rock hardness—hard enough and strong enough to walk on without crumbling. Riphath's mind was immediately alive with possibilities. The building of shelters and dwellings was backbreaking and labor-intensive, as stone was quarried and shaped then transported and placed to make walls. To Riphath, this hardened mud suggested a thousand possibilities. A new technology was being conceived. This new medium could be molded at site into easily handled sizes and perhaps even shapes, but other problems would need to be solved. Large blocks of quarried stone, if well finished, sat securely one on the other under their own weight, needing little or no bonding. Smaller, lightweight blocks, or bricks, not having the density of stone, would require another medium to bond them together.

The problem kept Riphath awake for some nights. Resin from trees might work but was nowhere near plentiful enough. A group of womenfolk searching out the best water supplies had spoken of a strange phenomenon at one end of the plain, where a warm dark-red-brown substance in abundance oozed to the surface, creating large, unsightly ponds. The inventive man had to satisfy his curiosity. The substance was thick and sticky with a pungent odor. Some of the people had encountered it before.

What Riphath, the observant one, noticed was that while the warm substance at the center of the pond, where it seeped and bubbled from the ground, was quite liquid, that which now lay at the extremities had solidified, creating a kind of dam over which new cooling material crept. Again, Riphath's mind leaped ahead, but it also ran back to the stories of his father, who told him of their great ancestor, Noe. Had he not used such a substance in the immense vessel he and his sons had built to carry life across the great deluge? Surely this could work.

IAN HEARD

The pitch was readily accessible, could be carried in vessels to each site, kept warm over fires, and simply applied between courses of newly baked bricks, quickly to cool and harden, not only acting as the bond but also preventing moisture from migrating vertically or horizontally from brick to brick. The ancient record says, "They used brick instead of stone and tar for mortar." Now there was more than just the alluring appearance and atmosphere of the plain to engender optimism; there was a technology driver as well. Yachim too was well pleased, and the wishful rhetoric of the day they first viewed the plain took new wings.

It was Yachim's wife who, as only wives can, drew his attention to the fact that the new driver seemed to be overtaking his attitudes and even his persona. She reckoned that he only saw the possibilities opened by the new technology as opportunities for self-aggrandizement. Women! He brushed aside her observations as of no account. He spoke as a man with a vision, a man on a mission. Yachim was given to enthusiasms, most of them harmless enough, but this one did seem to overrun him; it seemed to take on a life of its own.

To all and sundry, he had begun to say, "Look at this. Do you see what this means? This will help us make something great for ourselves and of ourselves. Indeed, we must. We must build and not just our dwellings, but we must create an edifice that reflects our new ability to overcome obstacles. A monument to new possibilities, to ourselves! A city, yes, let's

THE PLACE

build a city with a tower that reconnects us with the cosmos and with meaning and speaks of our destiny. This will be known as our arrival, as the place where we rediscovered truth and power and meaning, where our disappointments vanished once and for all, where the hollowness some speak of was vanquished, where New Man, Replete Man, was born!"

He received applause for that, and he feigned modesty.

Too, city and tower would provide the answer to that other contributor to the hollowness, that engendered by the land itself; for that unwelcome sense of aloneness that vast emptiness of land with unimpeded sky above and the awful unknown stretching away to vague and uncertain horizons gave rise to. His wife had expressed that so well herself. Surely answers lay in the security offered by centralization and corporate achievement around city and tower rather than fragmentation into that emptiness. That would just mean further aloneness and loss of selfhood.

"The reason we need to do this," Yachim rationalized, "is lest we be scattered abroad over the face of the whole earth and become weak in fragmentation. Together we can be mighty and safe and protected and accomplished."

His words surprised even himself. He was surprised but pleased by his own strength of conviction. His hearers applauded both him and his words. This was a new enjoyment that gave him a sense of invincibility and a curious pleasure. In the quietness of the night, Yachim could hear his strong words replayed in his subconscious, but not with any detachment or objectivity, not with any critical analysis or self-examination. All was clear to him; the new age was dawning, and he and his family were part of it—no, authors of it! This was something for which, ever after, he and the generation he led would be immortalized. The euphoria was contagious. Yachim was not a man to speak tentatively. His demeanor and enthusiasm now inspired ambition and confidence. Nor was he a man to suffer fools or pessimists. They surged forward on a wave of promise as the new bricks, city, and tower leaped into reality.

If any shadow of doubt about his demeanor or attitude in this venture or about validity of motives ever flitted about the edges of Yachim's consciousness, it was quickly dispatched. Only his wife doubted, but she had always been a pessimist.

"Yachim, don't you think you're rushing things a bit?" she ventured and later said, "Yachim, remember we were told that father Noe of old said we must always seek Creator's ways, and the reason the great deluge came was because people did not, but were full of prideful ideas and independence. Don't you think we should take his example? His first thought was not how to make a name for himself. In fact, he worshipped Creator and planted a vineyard after the deluge, and Creator made the ground bring forth rich produce."

Clever and euphoric Yachim had an answer: "Yes, and then he got drunk on its wine and disgraced himself, so big deal! I'll build a city and a tower, and everyone will benefit!"

THE PLACE

Then in a quiet evening moment, his wife said, "Yachim, tell me honestly why you really want to do this thing...I have to say I'm uncomfortable about it. Believe me, I want an end to the hollowness and the lessness that I feel, but, you know...what you said about not being scattered, that, well...doesn't that sort of contradict what father Noe said Creator told him about multiplying and filling the earth?"

Inwardly Yachim hated that kind of painful logic from his wife. It always took several hours with his peers to quiet such feminine folly. She should simply fulfil her duties, forget her feelings, and accord him the respect due such a great emancipator. Women were not made for innovation and adventure, his peers assured him; they are always tentative and difficult about new things. Never mind, she would soon settle down when the new life opened its gates and doors to them. She'd look back on the old days and be glad they had been delivered from all that. After all, it was she herself who had said, "When will we find what you're looking for, and when will our hearts be full?"

Yes, that's really what I am, Yachim mused one night, *an emancipator*; the idea or impression seeming to come from without, impinging on his consciousness, uninitiated yet comfortably, subtly assuring and growing larger as he nurtured it. *Yachim-Pathach—more than he who establishes. Yachim the Emancipator. Yes, it's fitting.* He feigned appropriate modesty as he nodded in acknowledgement to himself. *If I bring the people into something they're longing for,*

I deserve recognition for that. Perhaps there could be a modest monument or a likeness in the center of the city, or would it look better at the base of the tower?

These thoughts he did not share with his wife. Milcah would not be able to fully appreciate his forward-thinking and largeness of vision. *Later she would see it,* he self-assured. Riphath would, and so, in time, Yachim-Pathach would share them with one who was truly a man of discernment. Indeed, a plaque or inscription in recognition of Riphath too would be quite appropriate; not as prominent as his own but nonetheless an expression of due and proper appreciation.

Yes, it was coming together now, and the people were with him, of one accord, one mind. Creator—if indeed there was such a reality—after all, that which they had now embarked upon was what was tangible, real, and rewarding; Creator could only be congratulatory of such initiative and enterprise. Would not Creator, if anyone, appreciate this new creation, rising as it was from the heart of those made in his image? Would he not expect his creation to find its way out of the pervading hollowness and any other problem? Surely it was Creator who had placed within man the capacity to find and make his way to his own salvation. Yes, the way forward and out was clear.

Birth of an Ideology

There are few limits to what people of one heart and mind can accomplish. On September 12, 1962, the world marveled as the president of the United States of America, John F. Kennedy, unfurled the vision to put man on the moon. "We choose to go to the moon, and we choose to do it in this decade," he said. To some he might as well have said, "We choose to turn into pumpkins," but the vision captured the heart and mind of the American people, and they did it.

Optimism prevailed in Shinar too. A new technology emerged. Bricks and mortar opened a far less burdensome way to permanence than quarrying and moving stone or even using random stones. There were abundant supplies of the mud and the tar. Searching was over, and a new sense of belonging and connectedness could emerge through the making of an edifice larger than themselves, created by energies derived from the very yearnings within. As water was to thirst and food to hunger, this would surely be to those deep-in cries. They gave it birth—how could it not be? Man's new creation would, in turn, recreate him; he would be a new being, strong, connected to whatever larger purpose may exist, secure and replete.

City and solidarity would provide the sense of belonging and security so longed for. It would put an end to conflict, ushering in an era of spellbinding mutuality and cooperation. In addition, tower would provide significance as well as connectedness to the heavens above where sun shone and from whence rain now came—connectedness to the greater world, the visible universe, where one they knew of called

Creator dwelled, and of whom their first father, and Noe after him, had spoken. Man could now become a being of great creativity and repute. Through self-effort, reconnection to Creator and salvation from the dogging hollowness would be achieved. The credit would be man's own.

It sounded too good to be true, and it was, but a doctrine was born.

Invention, discovery, and technology were the drivers of these people then. For many, they remain the drivers today, for as then, every discovery, invention, or advance carries within it two competing seeds. One seed, which can be chosen for germination, is the capacity to excite optimism, to flatter mankind and to tease into greater commitment to the cause of self-salvation—man as his own messiah. The other seed, if chosen, will be planted—yielded—in worship before the Almighty with thanksgiving and recognition of how little and finite is our knowledge and with the prayer for Him to take the seed and cause it to grow into something productive that brings greater and greater fame to Him and greater willingness in us to work in cooperation and partnership with Him.

The new doctrine tantalizingly held out the offer that at last, if not finding the answer within themselves to the hollowness, they could manufacture it themselves from their expanding intellectual and creative activity; to at last touch and reconnect with, by their own hand, the source of repleteness and even immortality, if not eternality. It was strong doctrine, for it continues to our day, espousing the idea that man has, within, the ability to solve every problem of conflict, famine, disease, and death. It preaches that problems not yet surmounted will eventually be by dint of cleverness, invention, and evolutionary improvement. It is committed to the path of self-improvement of personal, social, and environmental conditions, out of the noble, life-giving resources of man's intellect and cooperation. The doctrine, born so long ago, is called humanism.

City and tower became a shining reality, monuments to the possible and declarations, indeed material evidence of the irrefutability of the doctrine. Bavel and its much-later successor, Bavylon, both momentarily represented what moderns call the triumph of the human spirit. But the triumph was short-lived.

A spirit of great cooperation and camaraderie had quickly seen planning, building, and completion of city and tower, and Yachim-Pathach's chest swelled with satisfaction and pride. The people extolled him and Riphath as the doctrine became mantra and took firm root in hearts and minds. Nothing would now be impossible for New Man.

And therein lay a problem.

The power of human accord can be extraordinary. When mutual benefit beckons—and, on occasions, for altruistic, even unselfish reasons—men and women are united, capable of phenomenal achievement. It is true that the product of an accord can be greater than the sum of its parts. The value of the product depends on motive. People cooperate for good as well as for evil. The essential elements needed for cooperative effort include mutuality of objective and motive. When facilitated by ease of communication and sharing of resources and knowledge, things get done—both for good and for evil. What could be wrong with this new demonstration of technological advance, human concord, and triumph over adversity?

But Creator was not impressed. The record shows that *He* deliberately thwarted this enterprise. Was Creator piqued? Miffed? Jealous? Capricious and mean? Why would the creatures' efforts at advancement and initiative not please Him and receive his imprimatur? Whatever was wrong that such advance should be met with such opprobrium? Surely if Creator desired the generations to come to believe in Him and worship and serve Him, would it not be appropriate for the record to show that their initiative received His approval? Indeed, it would be, if in fact the initiative *could* result in the eradication of the hollowness, but it could not. This Creator knew and custodian should have known. For *He* knew such actions were but another manifest expression of the autonomy that caused the hollowness and that they could only ever carry custodian further from repleteness!

Creator knew that unpartnered, independent action was the cause, not the remedy; the disease, not the cure. *He* knew that the completion craved could be found only,

THE PLACE

paradoxically, in surrender of self-government, to that which *He* offered. For His desire was a Creator-custodian partnership that would result in extraordinary productivity wherein custodian participated in Creator's master plan to bring creation to mature fullness. As extraordinary as the city and the tower may have been, their driver was the problem. Creator was not anti-cities or anti-towers, but He could not be *for* anything that was not able to answer custodian's crying need. That would make Him partner to the hollowness. *He* could not be. As it turns out, in fact, *He* already had in mind a city and a place—indeed, *the place*—for custodian, which could be gained in partnership, and it was one that could answer! *Shalom* was a part of its name, and it was to be where *He* would touch earth with the blessings of His realm. Had custodian listened and cooperated, he would have been shown the way to the city that answers.

There was a man who listened, and we will hear of him soon.

A vanity is something that fails to answer; a thing forever falling short of its promise. What Creator saw, as He observed, was no answer to the hollowness. He saw a vanity that had risen out of custodian's heart, without reference to Creator. Creator had designed his image-bearing creature for the same kind of repleteness that He enjoyed. Creator desired to nurture the creature into it.

What Creator saw as He visited was the sad potential for multiplied perversion of this kind as custodian spent himself seeking answers in further vain independence and misguided accord. He saw the tendency for deceived custodian to seek relief from hollowness by his own hand when it lay exclusively in the hand of Creator. What custodian did not want to see, though Creator desired to help, was the change for the worse that had occurred within as a result of the choice for independence in the garden from which he had been banished. It was a change that rendered him incapacitated and unable to break free from a now-embedded principle of futility. A part of that change too was the incurable hoax that an answer resided within the reach of the creature's own mind and will; a worship therefore, of creature rather than of Creator.

The garden had been the test bed for the Creator-custodian partnership. If misguided accord only led custodian deeper into a spiral of detrimental vanity, limitations would need to be placed on the capacity for such accord. Just as barred access to the tree of life earlier in custodian's history had placed limitations on custodian's capacity for evil, now a limit was needed for custodian's capacity for destructive cooperation, which led only to deeper hollowness. For man's own welfare, therefore, Creator brought a confusion that forced groups apart into less damaging isolation. Voluntary accord and partnership centered on Him and His big plan could bring health and shalom to all; accord centered on independence could bring nothing but more destructive futility with despair.

THE PLACE

The tower at Bavel was an expression of messianic pretension; a display of misguided zeal to solve a problem, to fill the farthest-in desires for belonging, significance, and security. So the tower suggestion was greeted with eagerness and expedited with great expectation so that custodian could, as he collectively said, "make a name for ourselves and not be scattered." The unfortunate motive was self-salvation. Tower and city was a declaration of autonomy; it was custodian following the dictates of a heart that by now, sadly, was deeply infected with the virus transmitted from collusion with Destroyer. It could only therefore lead away from, not to, the longed-for shalom.

Efforts at self-salvation only result in intensifying the problems they seek to solve; an intensifying of frustration and futility. The "salvation city and tower" custodian built with such gusto gave substance to what custodian's heart now contained—vanity. It was simply a representation, an image of the hollowness and lessness within.

A City Called Confusion

After the strange recent events, it was not easy for Yachim-Pathach to admit that his wife had been uncomfortably close to truth. He was fortunate that he and she were still of one tongue, if not of one mind. He had heard tell of some who no longer understood members of their own family. The "visitation" had been weird and had created enormous upheaval.

People awoke one day to discover a babble around them—the sounds of confused speech that could not be understood; the sounds of folks in desperate chatter, trying to make those near them understand, their own speech suddenly not comprehended by many around them. The visitation and its outcome became all-occupying and time-consuming and led to extreme frustrations and eventually to warlike tensions as people fought to exchange meaning. The confusion of language had not only suddenly shattered the dream but had totally fragmented the solidarity and combined enthusiasm that had seen the building of their great symbol of significance.

The social fabric and dynamic was in upheaval, and every routine of life was in chaos. Confusion reigned. People who could still communicate with each other eventually clustered into groups and cooperated but found it necessary to distance themselves from other groups to limit the pain and frustration and the opportunity for jealousy, rivalry, and outright warfare. It was awful, and Yachim-Pathach had been humbled by events suddenly beyond either his explanation or control. In fact, he had an unsettling and growing sense that the strange events were not at all unrelated to his and his followers' recent deeds. He was a somewhat chastened Yachim again, and since the great fragmentation, after which he could no longer make himself understood to his brother and comrade

THE PLACE

Riphath, Milcah was not hearing theories and assertions and grandiose schemes.

She ventured in that matter-of-fact way that always made Yachim cringe. "Seems to me that Creator has said that if confusion is your choice, then confusion you can have. Whether we like it or not, we have now been well and truly fragmented and scattered." Yachim was in no mood to engage her and, in any case, couldn't think of a clever answer, so he pretended to be very busy showing his only son how to make a stronger tent peg. They had decided to set up their family with several families whose tongue they could understand near a watercourse many days' journey from recent occurrences.

Bavel had not provided an answer to the hollowness, but Creator had in mind a place that could. Not a city-tower that rose from ground already blighted with futility, nor from the now-corrupted heart of custodian, and whose very name, Bavel (later Bavylon), became synonymous with confusion and vanity. The city birthed from the heart of Creator was a city of shalom soundness, with integrity and prosperity; a city that would have ultimate expression coming down from above yet having a temporal prototype on earth—Yerushalem! It was everything that Bavel was not. It was a city where Creator would again be enthroned on planet Earth and from whence His government and especially the benefits of that government would be made manifest.

Bavel and all "Babylons" have since attempted to escape the hollowness and lessness but instead have become further monuments to futility. They have all been symbols of custodian's self-governing arrogance, and every one of them has fallen. Each one is destined to fall, but men of pride and arrogance still go on building Babylons to make a name for themselves, hoping, vainly, to reconnect with significance, immortality, eternity. For what is actually in man's heart is the lost city, the garden city Creator had once provided. *City*, in its Hebrew meaning, is a guarded or watched-over place and therefore a place of permanence and security and provision. From the beginning, man has tried to reestablish what he'd lost, and so when Quayn went out alone, one of the first things he did was to build a city. The longing for *the city* remains in every heart.

Fortunately there are two stories in those early chapters of custodian's journey, contrasting stories, indeed two models: the one just narrated, which always ends in bitter hollowness; the second story is that of a better way that leads to life.

2

The Hint Out of Nowhere

A Legendary Place, a Legendary Person

Creator had his men and women scattered here and there. Just as there had been Chenokh (who walked with Elohim and was mysteriously taken by Him) and Noe, there were individuals and enclaves who found that seeking Creator and walking in cooperation with him brought great reward, dividend, and more importantly, shalom. But now such people were a courageous and blessed minority. Others, the majority, were again spiraling downward into an abyss of self-seeking, self-aggrandizement and self-pleasure, all the while believing or pretending that they were moving upward into self-actualization.

Once free from the thrall of anxiety that so seemed to define their existence, they would achieve an "arrival" in which they could self-congratulate. The hollowness (they contrived to believe) was being defeated. Men preached the doctrine of liberation from outdated and obsolete mores that inhibited progress and the advancement of culture. The new "freedom" manifested itself in free or exhibitionist expressions and excesses of every human appetite—food, wine, and intoxicants; sexual licentiousness of any and every kind; self-promotion and deceptive or corrupt dealings with each other, not to mention exploitation of relationships for personal ambition and ends. Could be lifted straight from the pages of almost any twenty-first-century newspaper!

The man Avram knew that nephew Lot was likely to get out of his depth as he pitched his tents near the cities of the plain of Yarden and eventually closer and closer to the city called S'dom. But Lot was young and, when given a choice by Uncle Avram, had made his decision for the well-watered plain. Here it was again, the understandable attraction of the plain country; this time Yarden Plain. But it was Yarden Plain with the cities of the plain, which included the already notorious G'morrha and S'dom, as well as Admah, Tseboiim, and Tsoar, where decadence and total self-interest had now become de rigueur. It was not long before Lot, while maintaining his integrity, found himself in deeper than he'd bargained for.

Avram also knew of a somewhat fabled place where an equally fabled person was said to dwell. The telegraph of travelers and trade and herdsmen ensured that stories

THE PLACE

crossed borders and territories and grew with the telling as they do in any age, only more slowly then than now. News was that he was one whose lineage no one could trace to anyone they knew, although there were those who believed him to be Noe's son, Shem. Yet this, so it was told, was a man of great bearing who spoke and acted with an authority that seemed to come from elsewhere. He made sacrifice to Elohim/El Elyon, and his dwelling place was known as Shalem, curious in its meaning as it was the very opposite of the hollowness that Avram knew haunted many people. Talk was that the place name, Shalem, had arisen because it best described the character and demeanor of its most revered occupant.

More mysteriously, there were those who said that the region and "the place" (as it was becoming known) were, in fact, the very site of the Beginnings; that before the deluge and all the changes to rivers and geography wrought by that extraordinarily catastrophic event, the area and the place now being known as Shalem was once the area of Edhen, where dwelled the first one, 'Dam. He was so named for the red soil of the region from which Elohim had formed him (the same terra rossa soil of Judea and Galilee in which wine is grown in our day). He lived there with Havveh, the woman, formed from a part of 'Dam in order to provide completion, and her name meant "life."

They had dwelled in a lush and plentiful garden named Gan Edhen, where Creator also could dwell and walk on earth. As all knew, the deluge had caused enormous upheaval and change to landscapes and to the river that once sprang and flowed from the region of Edhen. In those far-back days, it used to flow out from the region and broke into four separate rivers known as Pison, Ghikhon, Tiigra, and Ufratu , watering a vast and beautiful area. Both the Banishment and the deluge meant that few clues remained of what once had been, except for that spring and stream at Shalem called Ghikhon, it also being a sadly depleted vestige of its former self following the Diminishing.

But it was said by many that Creator still saw the place as the locus of His original plan for creation. They said that from the same place where origins had been spoiled, there would spring, as it were, a new River bringing a new creation and a new kind of life!

But would not such a new creation require, surely, a new 'Dam? Some even said that the one, Malkhi-Tzedek, might be that new beginning or a pointer to it? Perhaps. And would it not also require a new bride for the new 'Dam, by whose union the new creation could be generated? How could such things be?

Malkhi-Tzedek

To his wife, Sarai, one day, the man Avram voiced a desire. They had just given hospitality to travelers who had regaled them with much news from other parts, including that of an encounter with this Malkhi-Tzedek, whose wisdom

THE PLACE

and authority had left a lasting mark on them. It had, they said, brought to life within them a desire to follow the One, El Elyon, of whom he spoke and whose very presence and life seemed so mysteriously there, as an invitation to something—to repleteness and peace in Shalem.

"I would like to meet him. It's said that he is Shem, carrying forward the faith of his father, the great Noe of the deluge, and if what I hear of him is so, then I'm sure our hearts would be one. I'd love to tell him how Creator has made himself known to me and how that which I believed *He* said to me has been shown to be more true than anything I've ever known...and about what *He* has promised us and about Bayth-El and the place and—"

"Take it easy" was Sarai's interruption, and she laughed, as she often did, at what she called Avram's flights of fancy. She tried to keep up with his unshakable belief in what he said was Creator's direction. He said you could know it if you were serious about doing it once *He* made it known. He said that it was like walking in a partnership into purpose, and she had certainly seen the fruit. She had been prepared to go out on a limb with him, and it had to be Creator who had made it work. Of course, she knew his fallibilities too but was wise enough not to use the "Mitsrayim[1] thing" as any kind of weapon.

---

1. Ancient name for Egypt.

"You really know nothing about this man, except what some wandering herdsmen have said. They could be embellishing the story, as all travelers like to. Anyway, if Creator wants you to meet him, let him organize it."

Avram thought that was pretty good advice and kept silent about it, but just as with so many experiences he'd had with things Creator wanted his attention about, it seemed to stay front of mind; even after he'd laid it down and was busy with his work and his now-considerable household, livestock, and retinue.

It was time and seasons later—who can tell how long—when, in the usual spring skirmishes over trade routes and boundaries, several leaders of the above cities and lands subjugated by an alliance under Kdorla'omer of Elam, rebelled. They had been in subjection for some twelve years. In the resulting fracas, the alliance had prevailed and punished the rebellious groups, many of whom fled to the mountains, and some perished in the tar pits of Siddim. Kdorla'omer spoiled S'dom and G'morrha, carrying off all the goods and food. Nephew Lot and family were among the victims taken prey. However, as providence would have it, an escapee of Avram's people brought the bad news to Avram, who immediately raised a militia and went after the alliance. Surprising them by night, he recovered the people and the goods, and left the leaders dead and the alliance in disarray.

THE PLACE

It was at this point that an event of age-long and spiritual significance took place. The grateful king of S'dom arrived at Avram's place in the King's Valley of Sh'veh, close by the mysterious Shalem. While nephew Lot had been pitching his tents closer and closer to S'dom, Avram had been getting closer to the place, the mysterious place. And not only did the grateful king of S'dom turn up, but suddenly the one known as the priest-king from Shalem materialized, offering to Avram the symbols of oneness and blessing, bread and wine!

Sarai's words suddenly sprang into Avram's consciousness. "Anyway, if Creator wants you to meet him, let Him organize it."

So there were indeed other men of righteousness, and this one spoke a blessing over Avram with a strange but recognizable authority. He spoke of Creator as El Elyon, possessor of heaven and earth! "On Avram be the blessing of El Elyon, maker-possessor of heaven and earth, and blessed be that one El Elyon, whose protection has brought your enemies into your power."

The words impacted Avram so that he had a deep-in knowing that they came from one who was standing as proxy at that moment for the very one, El Elyon, of whom he spoke.

A response also welled up within Avram, and it too came from the One of whom Malkhi-Tzedek spoke. It called forth from Avram a desire to give, and so he gave to the priest-king a tenth of all that he had taken as spoil in the victory that Creator/El Elyon had given him.

And then he returned the balance to its rightful owners. The somewhat-stunned king of S'dom watched this strange transaction with curiosity, for the arrival of Malkhi-Tzedek and the timing of his words to Avram had wrong-footed him! Shalem hadn't been rescued by Avram! What on earth did it have to do with this man who showed up and pronounced a word of blessing over Avram and shared bread and wine with him?

"Look," says the bemused king of S'dom, expressing his gratitude. "Take all the goods for yourself and just give me back my people."

But to the amazement of the king, this man, Avram, is not interested and will not allow himself to be enriched by S'dom. "I've raised my hand in allegiance to El Elyon," intones Avram to the king of S'dom, from a position of strength due not just to S'dom's indebtedness to him but also to fresh revelation and perspective.

Such effect did the encounter have that Avram used the very name that Malkhi-Tzedek had used—Most High God, El Elyon! He even used the same description, "possessor of heaven and earth." In doing so, he demonstrated to whom his lot belonged and proved that his allegiance was impossible to divide.

Thus did Avram meet the mysterious Malkhi-Tzedek, and all that he had heard was verified. On reflection,

THE PLACE

Avram recognized how stunningly Creator/El Elyon had engineered the entire episode. It began to look more and more to him as though there was nothing, not one thing, outside the control of this one; that *He* was somehow able to work all things and all events to His own purpose and for the utmost good of those who walked His way!

This was new to Avram; the place Shalem, the man, and the name he used for Creator. Yhwh—Lord, he had known; the I Am who is and who causes. But this new name he warmed to, and it thrilled him. El Elyon—God, the Most High One! God of gods! The Supreme One! This was how Avram had just experienced *Him*—as the One in charge of everything! It is safe to say that there was a connection and a kinship in their hearts that was far more than human camaraderie. Avram thrilled, and his heart told him something deep was being transacted as they shared bread and wine. But there was something more; there was for Avram the mystery of the nearby place from whence this Malkhi-Tzedek came—Shalem. It was difficult to know if the mystique arose from the place or from the being, the man, the proxy, who had arrived at the strategic moment specifically to bless him. Something about the place had been planted in Avram's own deep place that day. If this man was an example of those who lived there, he would like to know more about it. Surely it was a place of spiritual significance, perhaps of deeper encounter with this one, El Elyon?

It almost gnawed at him, and such was the sense that Malkhi-Tzedek had been sent by Creator at that very moment; that this priest-king had stood in that moment as proxy for Creator, that Avram had given him the tenth of the spoil from the victory he knew Yahweh had given him.

Should it then surprise that the ancient annals show that following this event and Avram's response, Creator said to Avram, as he was then still known, "Don't be fearful, Avram. I am a shield for you as well as your increasing reward"? Creator had, a long time ago, chosen to prove the man's obedience by asking him to leave Charran's familiarity and security; now *He* had chosen to prove his allegiance. In response to the test of obedience, Avram had found that Creator led him to the new place just as He said He would. Now, in response to a test of Avram's allegiance, Creator locked in protection and reward. And now?

3

Yerushalem Man: Substance and Multiplication

Repleteness

The aging but not yet old man set a steady pace, walking as one on a mission as though drawn or compelled, his eyes undistracted. Close to sixty-five kilometers in two days over rough terrain was not bad going and spoke of something in the man's heart. It was now the third morning since the party of four—a father, a son, and two servants—had begun their journey. Like the son, the two menservants only speculated about the aging man's purpose. Youthful and adventure loving, they had grown fond of the man they served and to whom they were distantly related. They wondered at the resolution in the older man's demeanor, a resolution reflected in his unaltering gait. The three young men threw stones at the hares, wild goats, and donkeys they startled as they headed north along the barely discernable path. Occasionally their ass balked and brayed at a whiff of danger on the wind in the form of unseen lion or bear. They were curious about the split wood the ass carried and assumed it was for some kind of offering their master would make at Moriah, the destination he had indicated to them. They were not old enough to have seen him build an altar of stones and make offering before, but they would have been told of the place and also of Mamre, and they well knew of their master's devotion to Creator. They were the recipients of the patronage that Creator spoke of in His ever-present tense of eternity, when *He* described the man in the ancient record thus: "I have known him...that he will command his children and his household after him, that they keep the way of Yahweh to do righteousness and justice." Life in the security of the man's household was good for these young men.

But now, on this the third morning, the master's resolve coalesced in even greater firmness as he came in sight of the place within the hills they called Moriah. Here he instructed the two to wait with the ass while he and his son went on with the wood and the fire they had carried all the way from Be'er-Sheva. The young men's anticipation quickly soured to disappointment as they churlishly tethered the ass, but the father and master knew that their presence in what was about to unfold was not for them and could well prove a hindrance. All the master said was, "Wait here with the donkey while the lad and I go yonder and worship, and we'll be back."

Avram's weathered left hand, palm down, shielded eyes turned down at the corners (as those of a man who smiled frequently) against a new sun as it triumphed over austere hills to his north and east. The presence of the mountains of Moriah in his field of view—*the place*[1] to which *He* had directed him—carried into his belly a brief but potentially overwhelming sense of apprehension. He had seen them before; it was close by the territory of his exhilarating encounter with Malkhi-Tzedek, but now they seemed pregnant with strange foreboding, challenging his pledges to Creator's will and purpose, as they had so recently challenged the now surmounting sun.

The ripples of apprehension that made their presence felt in his belly kept him from breakfast. Had Creator perchance let him down? Worse, had Creator had a change of mood? Was *He*, like him, subject to whim and caprice? Come to think of it, was it actually *He* who had spoken? These are questions that, given half a chance and opportunity to take root, could grow tendrils that would coil like vines around his resolve and strangle it into debate, compromise, or capitulation.

---

1. Gen. 22:3, 4, 9, and 14 NKJV (Hebrew *ha makom*)

Faith's Gift

Yet no sooner had such thoughts attempted to make a claim than like the sun, something larger rose and shone within the aging man's breast, surmounting the potential mountains of fear, dispelling gloom and apprehension. Something else supplanted all his other emotions—tranquility!

It was a gift Creator planted within him. It was the knowing of faith that came from outside himself; it was assurance; it was certitude. And now *it* was in the belly instead, dispelling uneasiness and misgiving. The assurance that, just as he had looked ahead to the mountains, Yahweh, El Elyon too had looked ahead.

And the assurance began to metamorphose into an actual word that welled up within him to present itself in profound repetition so that he now found it upon his lips even as his son questioned, "Father...where is the lamb for the offering?" which was as well, for the thing Avram perhaps feared most was this question from his beloved son.

By now Yitzchaq's active mind had begun to question the leaving behind of the others and the lack of an object of sacrifice. He took comfort in his father's words to them, which had somehow strangely impacted him within: "Wait while the lad and I go yonder and worship, and we'll be back."

The word, beating now within Avram as though with his pulse, welled up onto his lips. It was "yireh, yireh, yireh"; in our language "foresight, foresight, foresight," "provision, provision, provision"; to see ahead!

THE PLACE

The meaning and the power of the word settled upon him so that he could see Yahweh wearing it as a mantle and as a title, Yahweh-Yireh, Lord of Provision, Lord who sees ahead! Every vestige of apprehension became engulfed by this tsunami word and was swept away by the truth of who this one truly is so that the aging man found himself replying to Yitzchaq's query in a voice so firm and calm that it surprised him: "Yahweh provides for himself the lamb for the offering."

And see ahead *He* did, and the man Avram was so borne along by the tsunami from his newly named partner and now seemed so unable to doubt what it would accomplish, that he knew with far-in certitude not experienced before that the One Seeing Ahead would bring Yitzchaq back from death—if necessary! At this moment, there was such a knowing planted from outside, within Avram's heart, that he knew, as he had never known anything, that he was moving in a partnership and an accord that *He* had initiated. It was an experience of union in which he understood that even such a provocative demand would come to make perfect sense. Avram sensed that it was a test for the ages, a prototype in hyperbole that would stand through the ages as a model for the partnership *He* desired for any who would walk out of the hollowness and into completeness. The One Seeing Ahead had unseen, prepared all. The great foreseer provided the ram at the right spot, at the perfect moment, mysteriously caught there in a bramble close by the altar upon which Avram had been willing to offer up the means to the fulfillment.

And so the man Avram gave the place his special name—"Yahweh will see and provide"—so that even though it already had significance, it now had specific significance to him and those destined to come from him. Both the place and the event it now represented began to be a byword in those days. The saying was, "On the mountain of Yahweh, it will be provided." It seemed to be prescient and pregnant with events and things not yet visible.

The walk back to the waiting party was a strange one, full of question. For the young lad Yitzchaq who trusted his father implicitly, there had been some moments of strangeness. Perhaps the curious binding of him was part of the worship ritual for the One his father called El Elyon and Yahweh, but when he was laid on that altar and saw his father stretch out his hand to take hold of the knife!—then came the voice indiscernible to Yitzchaq but arresting to Avram and the disclosure of the ram just behind him!

"Father, why did you put me on that altar when you knew the ram was there?" and "Father, what is so special about this place...why did we have to come here? Why couldn't we sacrifice back at Be'er Sheva?"

Avram skipped the first question. "I'll tell you about that one day when you're older, but let me tell you about the place. *He* has shown me that it is a place special to Him...the place of worship and sacrifice, for it is where our father 'Dam and his sons Qayin and Hevel made sacrifice

THE PLACE

to Him even after their expulsion from Gan Edhen. You'll remember how I told you of Qayin's sacrifice of fruit of his fields and Hevel's of a firstborn of his flock and how Qayin's heart was not good and Yahweh was not pleased?"

"Oh yes, Father," says the lad, now skipping unperturbed at his lighthearted father's side as he remembered the stories of many earlier evenings in the comfort of their large tent. "And Qayin became angry and killed Hevel, and Creator asked Qayin where his brother was, and Qayin said he didn't know, and anyway, what did it have to do with him, and Creator was angry and said, 'What have you done?' and Qayin walked away from Creator, and—"

"Yes, yes, you've got it," interrupted the father. "The important thing is the place. Remember *the place* because it is very important to *Him*—and to us!

It was later, when the lad had become a young man, that Avram told him more; much more, especially about multiplication. He told Yitzchaq how Yahweh had spoken a second time on that now-distant day on the hills of Moriah, at the place. He told Yitzchaq of the promise of multiplication. He explained that it was because he had been willing to lay down all visible means to multiplication and depend on Yahweh only that Yahweh had sworn: "Blessing I will bless you, and by multiplication I will multiply your descendants as the stars and as the sand, and your descendants will govern their enemies. In your seed, all nations on earth will be blessed."

"Yitzchaq, my son, if I have learned one thing, it is that at the place of His appointment, every need will be met." And to Avram's people, it soon became known as *the place*.

And these were sayings prophetically pregnant, for after a long, long gestation, Creator-Among-Us Himself became the greater provision, the substitute Ram caught in thorns on that same mountain. But that is later in the story of the One who is Lord of the place.

From Addition to Multiplication

There are those who say that the episode with Yitzchaq at the place at Moriah was a test of obedience for Avram, but this is not so. Years ago that same inner-conviction voice had urged Avram to leave Charran, a place called, in our tongue, Main Road, and to go to the place Yahweh would show him. In leaving, he had passed that test! He had gone out, leaving orthodoxy and conventional practice behind, trusting everything to Creator's voice and compulsion. There he passed the willingness-to-obey test.

Then some would say it was a test of allegiance, but not so. Allegiance had been proven at Shalem with Avram's "I have raised my hand to El Elyon" declaration. It was because of that declaration that El Elyon responded with, "Don't fear, Avram. I am your shield and great reward."

What need was there then for the man Avram, who had already walked in cooperation with Creator many days, to undergo some further lesson or probation?

THE PLACE

Did he who had been promised a son and was now enjoying the live presence and company of that promise need any reminding that Creator sees ahead and provides? Did Creator doubt he had this man's heart? Was there some deep insecurity in Creator needing the constant affirmation of Avram's devotion? Hardly! What manner of proving, then, was this? Yes, a test it was for Avram, but not primarily of obedience nor of allegiance. At the place, Creator chose to prove the man's dependence. Would Avram depend on Him to the exclusion of all other dependencies? It was a proving that marked the opening of a door to something greater, larger, and more expansive than dreamed. That greater, larger thing was a shift from the *addition* of a son to *multiplication* of a people; a shift from physical limitation to spiritual exponential. Its outcome would demonstrate for the generations that the hollowness could be banished, but only *His* way!

For to trust what can be seen (even when it's a present, tangible, and conspicuous answer to Creator's promise, as Yitzchaq was) is not to trust *Him*, but to trust something else—a thing that will prove to be a vanity. At Moriah, Avram's dependence was certified as cemented in the God of provision rather than in the provision of God. Deep inside, the aging man knew beyond a shadow of doubt that Yitzchaq was the promised seed, but ultimately, his faith must not be in the seed of God but in the God of the seed.

For to "fear" God is to have no other thing on which we depend or upon which we can even be tempted to depend.

No other gods. It is to hold Creator in such reverence that we would not dare offend; to have a relationship with Him that is not based on a wrong kind of fear, but which fears to offend, knowing that to offend Him is to damage self. This is the fear of the Lord that is the beginning of wisdom, and to properly fear God is to have no other thing from which we believe or even pretend it is possible to draw life, meaning, or purpose. Not even things He provided.

This was the lesson-test about what is empty and what is full, what is vain and what is life-giving, what is hollow and what is replete; about what is futile and what is fruitful. Vanity is to put our weight down on what has been given as though *it* was capable of carrying us into the full purpose of the Giver, but the key to productivity and multiplication is to rest all our weight only on the Giver. Yitzchaq could not be the source. It was at the place that Creator said to Avram, "Now I know that you fear Elohim...so blessing I will bless you, and multiplying I will multiply you."

At Bavel, custodian had turned to a vanity, but Creator was leading Avram on a walk away from vanity into the liberty of multiplication. The shackles of futility had to be broken. The demonstration began when Creator called this man to leave, in the obedience of faith, his country, his people, and his father's house for a land *He* would show him. The struggle to find the freedom was a lifelong one, but this was the man in whom Creator chose to demonstrate how a transfer of allegiance to Him was the path away from limitation. The place was part of the land to which Creator had called him and another step, a culminating step, in the process. *Moriah* means "selected by God," and it was where this man, Avram, was released into a new principle. At the place, every vestige of fealty to the principle of futility was broken. The aging man's dependence was not now on country or people or family, nor now even on the manifest son of promise, but wholly and solely on Creator.

These were the steps that made Avram, later called Ivrahim, the prototype of a new way of living. Those who would be known as his children will also be called to the place. It's a rendezvous for any who would stop trusting the sterile in order to find multiplication. Creator as the final and ultimate means to all ends is free to achieve His ends however He pleases, this way or that. He is able of stones—the very stones of the altar on which the manifest heir was placed—to raise up children to Ivrahim! There will be a Moriah to visit in order to absorb the truth about Creator in a way that helps us put all our weight down on it. Our Moriah may not be as portentous as Ivrahim's, but it will have life-lesson significance.

Ivrahim showed us the way!

Creator-Among-Us said as much many years later: "If anyone comes after me and does not hate his father and mother, his wife and his children, his brothers and sisters—yes, and even his own life—he cannot be my disciple."

The place and the event were a prophetic declaration of what was to come.

4

A Surprise for Yaakov at the Place

> And he encountered *the place.*
>
> —Genesis 28:11
> (The Hebrew verb used means to meet, encounter, come upon; emphasis added, *ba makom*)

"Mother," inquired the teenage boy. "Tell me again about what happened when Red and I were born." He used his twin brother's nickname.

Ribhqeh had a soft spot for the teenager. It showed in the way she coddled him and fussed over him. The other women noticed, and it gave them gossip fuel: "Red's the one who works. He's always bringing home wild game and field herbs, spends days and nights out there!" said Abigail to Bilhah one day as they walked to the well with the usual gaggle of village women in the cool of the day.

Bilhah agreed and added with a laugh, "Keep your eyes off him...I've got him earmarked for my daughter."

To Yaakov that day when he inquired, Ribhqeh said, "Look, strictly speaking, Red *was* firstborn, but he's just so independent and pays his mother so little attention." She sighed. "Heaven knows he and his father are as thick as thieves, but frankly, I'd be just as happy—happier—had it been you who came first." She touched her son's arm with fond assurance, and then she caught herself, realizing what she had just said and that it laid bare what was in her heart, so she made an attempt to temper it and to qualify it with, "Not that I have anything against Esav, it's just that I see more of you, and you care so for me...and Esav, well, he just does his own thing." And then, in self-justifying tone, "He's...well...he just seems so hard to get close to." Her own insecurity and need to be needed was showing, but she also knew the strange truth Yahweh had disclosed to her when she inquired about the jostling twins within her womb.

He had said, "Two nations, two peoples are within you, one people stronger than the other. The older shall serve the younger."

The barely suppressible jealousies and yearnings within Yaakov's heart came near the surface at such moments. Wild and treacherous inklings of how different everything might be, if only...

Ribhqeh too harbored foolish and even baneful thoughts at times, and so it was not that difficult when opportunity seemed fortuitously to present itself to aid and abet Yaakov in a pitiable deception of father Yitzchaq, now in his decrepitude.

The great annals reveal that it happened something like this:

Red had had a particularly engaging hunt, but he returned with his small retinue on the point of exhaustion. In an effort to beat the dying sun, they had walked some long hours without food. As Esav entered the family enclave, the smell of freshly cooked stew greeted his famished frame. Brother Yaakov had been cooking up a pot of the great soupy stew he often made, with some of the meaty bones of the beautiful young buck that Esav had taken a week back.

"Praise be to Yahweh, my dear brother," the famished Esav sighed as the aromas of herb and meat and lentil laid claim to his nostrils and his belly. "You must have known I'd arrive right now and give anything for stew."

"Oh yeah?" said Yaakov, not understanding why he resented Esav so deeply. "Just what is a big bowlful worth?"

Esav laughed and said, "Come on, brother of mine. Don't mess with my head. I've got to eat before I keel over. Don't kid around!"

"I'll tell you what," said Yaakov, with that thing that was always just beneath the surface now welling up to take opportunity. "I've worked hard at this, and you often enjoy the fruit of my culinary skills. How about a bowl of the best of this in exchange for that birthright you're always telling me is really nothing?"

"To be honest, right now, I could let it go just like that." Red clicked his fingers. "What's it mean anyway? Some old custom our parents and grandparents placed great store in. Puh!"

"A deal then?"

"Sure, a deal. Now be quick before I keel over." And with that, Esav valued his birthright as no more than the gratification of the need of the moment. His retinue drew a collective breath. Had they heard correctly? They were witnesses to a transaction that carried immense import. In such a devaluation, Esav was at once showing disdain for what Creator had prepurposed to be Esav's and was stepping away from the honor, responsibility, and privilege that should have crowned his life. Yaakov, of course, was required to accept the position and purpose given to Esav with grace, but he knew his twin well enough by now to know that it meant nothing to him. Even so, it was not Yaakov's to covet; how Red handled his responsibilities was for Red to answer for, both to his father and to the One who purposed it.

Now all that Yaakov had to do was figure out a way to get the firstborn's blessing from sinking Yitzchaq. Here Yaakov's scheming mother had a plan. She too resented the fact that Red did not appreciate what was his and she favored Yaakov. Now since Esav had treated the privilege so dismissively and it now belonged to Yaakov, why should not the dying favor and prophetic promise-words of Yitzchaq be spoken over him instead? It was only reasonable, she considered.

The way was opened, and a scheme took form when not too many days later, she overheard Yitzchaq call Red to him and make request for his favorite savory food of wild game from Esav's skillful hand.

"How long I have, I don't know," Yitzchaq said to Esav, peering at his form through eyes whitened and near unsighted by age and sun. "Go and return that I may eat and bless you in the presence of Yahweh before I die."

Deception offers primed moments. This was one, and no sooner was Esav well out of sight than Ribhqeh got very busy, instructing Yaakov to quickly take two choice kids from their flock with which she would prepare Yitzchaq's dish. The scheme would then involve Yaakov posing as Red to present the food to Yitzchaq to receive his father's blessing. The matter of Esav's hirsute arms and body could be dealt with by using the kid skins tightly wound and bound to his arms and neck, should Yitzchaq's suspicions be aroused. He could wear Red's best clothing.

"My son, you've returned so soon from the hunt!" said the ancient but still alert Yitzchaq.

Said the pretender, "Yes, Father, because Yahweh, your God, brought it into my hands for you."

Somewhat confused, Yitzchaq believed he heard the voice of Yaakov but felt the arms and smelled the smell of Red. "Are you truly my son Esav?"

"Father, I am." And to distract his mind from any lingering uncertainty and to close the matter as quickly as possible, he said, "Here, enjoy the beautiful food while it is warm and so full of flavor."

So Yitzchaq ate and called the pretender near, and smelled the smell of field and outdoors, of Esav, and kissed Pretender.

"May Elohim give you the dew of heaven and the fatness of the earth, of grain and wine. Let peoples serve you and nations bow to you, and be master over your brethren. May all who curse you be cursed and all who bless you be blessed." And with that, Pretender left as hastily as he could.

What a deathbed trauma for dear Yitzchaq. What an anguish of heart for Esav ensued. For soon after Pretender's exit, Esav arrived home, full of anticipation and cheer. He prepared the dish and came to present it to his father, and I leave it to the reader's imagination to envisage the scene, so full of pathos, outrage, and loss, that followed. Two sons—one a fool, the other a cheat.

And Red added this to his folly: "When my father has gone and we've mourned him, I will kill Yaakov."

The path of a cheat is not smooth. For a start, the conscience does not rest, and any satisfaction arising from all manner of contorted justifications is fleeting. This cheat, Yaakov—or Jacob, as we would call him—was no exception; for not only did he run from the one whom he had cheated, he also tried to run from his dogging conscience, and yet, running, found himself in a place of

THE PLACE

which he vaguely knew and found himself in the presence of Creator, Elohim, El Elyon, Yahweh, Adonai—the One from whom none escapes.

The position of favor had been so nearly his, except that as the twins presented at their birth, Esav had strangely usurped Yaakov's position. He knew so because his mother, Ribhqeh, divulged that the pair had jostled and rolled within her womb, and then Yitzchaq, his father, had named him Yaakov, "heel grasper"! The very name carried a stigma and a certain shadow of shame—someone who took advantage of others, a user. Long ago Yaakov had formed the conclusion that he had been gazumped by brother Esav and that the birthright had been unfairly taken from him by a twist of fate.

The Place Meets Yaakov

Isra-El's scribes and scholars know where Yaakov went when he fled his brother's wrath. On his way to Uncle Laban's place in the plain of Aram, where Ribhqeh hastily sent him, Yaakov found himself by design or by default at a location that had already become known as the place. Indeed, the ancient Hebrew writing calls it so, though many have been satisfied in translating it as "a certain place." The Hebrew (anglicized) says, "Vayifga ba makom" meaning "he encountered *the place* [emphasis added]." The scholars say that the definite article shows that it was a well-recognized location. It was the same place of which it is written that Ivrahim, on his journey with the young Yitzchaq, "lifted up his eyes and saw the place afar off". And then it was written that they had journeyed on together and that they had come to the place!

On a nonurgent journey, a man on a donkey or camel could travel somewhere between thirty-five and forty-five kilometers on a good day on a good track, with good provisions. Yaakov was in a hurry to put as much distance in as short a space of time as was possible between himself and an enraged Red. Traveling anxiously north from Be'er Sheva for a long day, Pretender Yaakov covered some sixty kilometers and found himself upon sudden sundown at the place! (As we have said, whether by design or by default, we are at a loss to know, as the language of the record indicates that he came upon it, as by accident). Methinks by default on his own part, but by design of the Great Other!

Arriving, just as light faded, he perhaps did not fully appreciate the significance of his arrival here. The nearest settlement to where he halted was known by others as Luz. It was a little more than a protective wall around a spring, but where he wearily stopped is the place so often mentioned by Father Yitzchaq and Grandfather Ivrahim. In the sense of Hebrew thinking, Yaakov had been here before—while in the loins of his father, Yitzchaq.

Although not mentioned in the annals, water was here, bubbling out from a spring on the eastern side of a hill, enabling him to water his beasts and the retinue with him. There was here also a strange and numinous awe. The sun-

THE PLACE

warmed stone he arranged as headrest was quite probably one of the very stones Grandfather Ivrahim had used on that "day for the ages" and upon which Yaakov's father, Yitzchaq, had been laid in surrender. Here Pretender was, in a particular location on the hills known as Moriah, but known by his family and people more reverentially and respectfully as the place!

Although tired from his journey, his mind was electric with recent events, and so he slept, at first fitfully but then more deeply, and dreamed a dream befitting the place! For what Yaakov saw was a terraced ramp, the record says, "whose top reached the heavens," connecting earth with heaven and with Yahweh Himself standing above it. And the holy messengers used the ramp to move between earth and heaven and heaven and earth; they were ascending and descending using the terraced ramp!

And later from somewhere deep within Yaakov, when he reflected on the dream, surfaced the memory of stories heard at his father's knee, of just such a terraced ramp, whose top (it was boasted) would reach the heavens, built in far-back days by his forebears. It was, he was told, an attempt made by men who felt empty to connect the two realms in the hope of escaping the thing they called the hollowness. That terraced tower had come from the ground up. It had come from the heart of man. It had come from the independence that had caused the hollowness. It failed to be a conduit to *Him*. It could not be used by the holy messengers who did His bidding. It could not do what Creator alone could do, and it had, therefore, been destroyed, it was said, by Creator Himself.

Yet here was the real connection—at the place! Not from below, not from the hollowness, but from above; indeed, from the fullness and made by *Him* and graced with His messengers' feet!

And Yaakov exclaimed, "How awesome is *the place*! This is none other than the Bayth-El and the very gate of heaven... and he called *the place* Bayth-El"[1] He had a sense that he was being shown something that had, in fact, always been there, though not visible—the stairway connection that belonged to Yahweh, not to the creature—but it was there! There it stood! This was *the place* indeed! Not created by creature in an empty attempt to escape the hollowness. What a vanity that was; what an act of arrogance, when the real means of connection existed all along! The bridge to the heavens and the possibility of access to heaven's fullness to swallow up the hollowness didn't have to be built up from the ground; it was always being provided by Creator. It had to be believed and received, not built. It came down from heaven, and above it stood Yahweh Elohim!

---

1. Genesis 28:16-19 paraphrased excerpts from Scripture4All interlinear Bible with emphasis added (ba makom and ha makom).

THE PLACE

Yaakov shivered and trembled within the shock and flood of revelation and understanding, and the shame and guilt over his jealous behavior began to shrivel and die.

At the place, Yahweh made a promise to the awestruck (and unworthy) Yaakov. It was just like the one given to grandfather Ivrahim. It concerned land and people and provision and multiplication, and it concerned *His* presence with Yaakov, who made from the pillow a pillar of remembrance and anointed it with oil. And Yaakov called *the place* Bayth-El; in our language, "house of God." He said, "This stone, which I have set up as a pillar, shall be Bayth-El, and of all you give me, I will give a tenth to you."

Yaakov said it at the place where Grandfather Ivrahim had also been moved to give a tenth to Yahweh's mysterious proxy, Malkhi-Tzedek.

Ah, there was indeed something awesome and special and holy at *the place*. It was becoming the Locus and the name Yaakov gave to it, like Ivrahim before him was a description of what he experienced, just as today we might affectionately call a place "engagement bay" or "birthday creek." It must be noted that the annals say he (Yaakov) called that place Bayth-El. Others knew the location as Luz. (It seems another nearby settlement to the north was also later given the name Bayth-el, as we shall see. We shall differentiate them as Bayth-El and Bayth-el.)

But this encounter was at Luz, on an eastern ridge of Mount Moriah, right against what had also been known as Shalem, and the reason for settlements there was the presence of a spring, which issued year-round with what people knew as "living water"—water that ever sprang and flowed from deep beneath the earth. It became known as Bursting Forth (*Ghikhon* in their language). Even Yaakov, as he was dying, said that El Shaddai had appeared to him at Luz because that is the name by which his sons knew it; but for Yaakov, it was now and forever Bayth-El, house of Elohim, and the place where His presence touched earth and made a gateway to heaven.

A day came, a much later day, when Yaakov (now named Isra-El by the One who dealt with him and with his treacherous character) blessed his own twelve sons. One, Yosef, had been his favorite. As Isra-El pronounced his dying blessing over Yosef, he remembered the spring, and he remembered the stone he had taken from the very altar stones of Ivrahim and had set up as a pillar so long ago at the place, and he spoke over Yosef:

"Yosef is a fruitful bough...a fruitful bough by *a spring*. His branches run over the wall. Archers have grieved him and shot at him with hatred, but his bow remained his strength, and his hands and arms were supple and strong by the mighty God of Yaakov, from whence is the Shepherd and *the Stone* of Isra-El."[2]

---

2. Gen. 49:22–24 Author's translation using Scripture4All interlinear Bible. Emphasis added.

THE PLACE

There were those who later believed that the Stone of Isra-El was the "Rock" that was taken with the people Isra-El into Mitsrayim and, after their release, accompanied them through the wilderness on their long and delayed journey to their promised land.

5

Seek the Place!

> Then there will be *the place* where the LORD your God chooses to make His name abide
>
> —Deuteronomy 12:11
> (NKJV, emphasis added, *ha makom*)

> - You shall seek *the place* where The LORD your God chooses ... to put His name for His dwelling place; and there you shall go.'
>
> —Deuteronomy 12:5
> (NKJV, emphasis added, *ha makom*)

The two silhouetted figures atop the summit, looking down and northwest over the plain of Yarden, or Jordan, as we call it in our language, were clearly in animated and even excited conversation. To the tribes below and behind them in the opposite valley to the south and east, they were no strangers, for they had known them these thirty-eight and more years. One of the two men was 120 years old, yet his vigor and acuity was like that of the much-younger man with whom he talked.

Cast across his face was a shadow, not of external light and shade. It was a shadow that came from within, as though of a disappointed yearning, but he brightened at the enthusiasm writ large on the features of the younger man, whose name, appropriately, it now seemed, was "the one who saves"—Yeshua.

As we pull our lens (as it were) from panorama to close-up and turn up the sound sensitivity, we hear the older man say, "Seek the place, Yeshua. That is what *He* said is important. Seek the place. I have reminded them of all the decrees and desires of Yahweh and that *He* said that when you cross over Yarden and dwell in the land, then there will be the place Yahweh, your God, chose to make His name dwell." He paused as a majestic golden eagle soared along the escarpment, only its wingtip feathers making minor adjustments. "As you have experienced so well, to please Him is to prosper your way." It had become a self-evident truth to the young man, and both of them wondered at the obstinacy and independence they had so often seen and experienced in the tribes and which always resulted in chaos or defeat or tragedy.

THE PLACE

As they both watched the effortless flight of the eagle, the younger man realized that Moshe's cheeks were glistening with fresh tears. Yeshua turned away again, not wishing to embarrass Moshe, who then spoke, and his words explained his emotion. "A long time ago, *He* told me to remind the people that He carried them on eagle's wings to Himself."

Moshe repeated the words, like a mantra, "Seek the place and keep the words. Seek the place and keep the words. *He* told me that the place is where He has chosen to put His name for His home! Can you believe that, Yeshua?"

Yeshua nodded. "I do, and I will," and then a question: "Did *He* mean that the people could only revere and worship Him at the place and there only? How can that be when we are to possess and dwell in all this vast and beautiful land we see below?"

"Ah, no," responded Moshe. "For *He* has told me that if the place is distant, you may make sacrifice and worship within your gates. How good Yahweh is to His people! No, the reason for the place is for an identifying locus and heart. We are the people of the one God who carries us on wings like that eagle." As was customary among his people, he gestured in its direction with his heavily bearded chin, and his undimmed eyes, now tearless, followed its effortless trajectory. "We are not as the Goyim who make gods that they have to carry." Moshe chuckled at the irony of it. Yeshua loved it when the old man talked such talk.

"The place is to signify that *He* is but one and chooses to make His home at a location that reminds us that He is among us...with us. It's a locus, like the tent He gave us for the journey. It stood right there in the middle of our camp to unify and focus us, to signify His nearness, His accessibility, His concern for us, and to keep us mindful of His watchful eye." And then the older man added, as one with fondness, "Remember, Yeshua, how you used to linger at the first tent I made, where we used to go away from the camp to seek Yahweh? Sometimes we couldn't drag you away! *He* had His hand on you way back then, and that's why you're here today!"

Yeshua felt the intended warmth and the affection in the old man's voice and words. The eagle made another sortie along the ridge, and a flutter of smaller birds appeared trying to harass the great bird, to no avail. A cloud that had momentarily clad the sun moved westward on the lazy breeze until the lowering sun found some holes through which it shot arrows of stark light. The arrows found their targets on streams and small lagoons across the plain as well as on Yarden River itself, and then on some snow that still clung tenaciously to a few slopes. The shining sight, by contrast, served momentarily to darken the shadow on Moshe's face, but as Yeshua spoke again, it lightened.

"My father." He used the familial term with deepest admiration and affection and, indeed gratitude, for the great man had been his spiritual patriarch. "It is the will of

THE PLACE

Yahweh, praised be His great name, to let you see it from afar. I too am saddened that the incident at the rock has brought this response from Him, but I want you to know that it has served a strong purpose. If *He* with whom only you have spoken face to face has dealt so with you, it has served to warn me that I must never act rashly or presume upon Him! For the people's sake and indeed for own His name's sake, *He* must be consistent." Then he added, "Aba, I am afraid."

Moshe said, "Remember, my son, our song from long ago? 'You will bring them in and plant them in the mountain of your inheritance, in the place you have made for your dwelling.' And remember the song *He* gave me just days ago—the song that has been growing in my heart these forty years—and what I said to you then before the people? It was, 'Be strong and of good courage, for you will bring the people into the land, and I will be with you.'" He looked into Yeshua's deep brown eyes, "What did *He* say, my son?"

"I will be with you," repeated Yeshua. And at once, the words just spoken settled on him just as tangibly as if Moshe had thrown his cloak over him. It was just like the old times when he lingered at the tent. *He* was there! The great eagle did one more traverse along the ridge and then soared heavenward and away.

IAN HEARD

"At last I see it," said Moshe. With a sigh, he continued, "What could have taken but eleven days has taken us forty years!"

6

Yeshua, Bayth-El, and Ay

Given God's instruction to "seek *the place* where the Lord your God chooses to put His name for His dwelling place" (Deut. 12:5 NKJV emphasis added), it can be reasonably assumed that Joshua would be eager to proceed into the land with that objective a priority. The search by archaeologists in our times has led to confusion and alternative proposed sites for ancient near-east settlements of biblical significance. Perhaps none more so than Bayth-El and Ay—Bethel and Ai. It is the conviction of your writer that the terrain surrounding Yerushalem provides an explanation that better fits the ancient narrative and that Ai stood just a few kilometers east of the true Bayth-El, or Jerusalem. The story proceeds on the basis of this explanation: perhaps Ay was near where Ma'ale Adumim stands today, just seven kilometers to the east of Yerushalem.

IAN HEARD

A Prostitute Moves in a New Direction

The two men thought they had slipped pretty much unnoticed as itinerant traders through the gate of the city. To further disguise their identity and intentions, they engaged, as did many itinerants, a lodging provider and harlot who sat just within the gate of the walled city. Rahav happily led the men to her quarters built into the shade and coolness of the high, thick walls of Yeriho. She was an astute and observant woman who detected something about the men from their speech, manner, and demeanor. Although their language was hers, there were differences in some pronunciations, inflections, and the words they used that provided clues to their possible origin.

"Have you come far today?" Her question was the first of a series that she intended to lead to a disclosure, for the woman, because of her profession, had already heard the stories and rumors of the vast company of people waiting in the plains just east of River Yarden, near the area they called the Meadow of the Acacias. Too, she had more than a passing interest in the God of these people, about whom she had heard much. What she had heard resonated with a certain yearning within, for she believed that there must be a true because there seemed to be so many untrue gods. She reasoned that if there was a thirst, its answer was clear, clean "live" water, not brine nor sulfur water.

"Have you come from the river?" she questioned, pointing east with her defined and pretty chin as she led them to a

THE PLACE

sparely furnished room with a small window in the great wall, looking out in the direction of the river of which she spoke. The day was almost spent, and the dwelling, being on the eastern wall, was already in deep shadow and cool. She hurried about, brought in a flaming brand from her cooking fire, and lit a lamp before she dipped a vessel into a large clay jar and poured them water. "They tell me there is a vast company just beyond Yarden led by one, Yeshua, and they are intent on possessing this land. I have heard about the God of this people and what has happened to the cities and the kings of the east, Og and Sihon, and I can tell you that fear has fallen on the whole land."

She did not seem interested in extracting money from them for her personal services beyond her fee for lodging, nor did these men seem interested in those services. In fact, although she was dressed and made up for her trade, she had a certain dignity, charm, and forthrightness that the spies found quite disarming. There was an unspoken and tacit agreement that lodging was all they sought.

The men made their responses as vague as possible. "We knew about their camps but avoided them. What is going on? What have you heard? Is this city well armed, or are we in danger?" They too were probing.

"To tell the truth," she continued, "the God they speak of sounds like the one I'd like on my side! Heaven knows I've prayed enough to any and all of our gods to give help to me and mine. The God they speak of is reputed to be the one who opened the sea and brought them out of Mitsrayim! It's been talked about around here for years…by people who say it's really true."

And then this, "By the way, did you see those soldiers eyeing you off when you came with me?"

Eliav's and Nahshon's hearts both missed a beat or two, for, trained as they were, they had not noticed what the woman, who was now their host, had seen. The men exchanged quick glances, each hoping the other would know how best to respond. They need not have worried, for Rahav, in a quiet and persuasive tone, then said, "Look, I think you've come from that camp, and, if so, want you to know I'm not going to betray you. If this is true, I want a deal." She was indeed a shrewd woman, but, of course, they could still not be certain of her motives and intentions, but before they could feign ignorance, she went on. "I want you to swear to me by your Yahweh that you'll be kind to me and my family in return for me giving you help." Rahav knew how to drive a bargain. "Give me a sure sign that you'll spare the lives of my father and mother, my brothers and sisters, and all who belong to them—and that you will save us from death."

"The terror of you has fallen on us so that inhabitants of the whole land are fainthearted and afraid." Prostitutes both received and gossiped all the news readily. Part of the trade was the exchange of money for pretended intimacy and comfort and a hearing ear, calculated to make a client feel valued and desired. Rahav continued, as one in whose heart was the desire for better things; who, having heard of the exploits of Isra-El's "Yahweh," had experienced a growing certainty that *He* was the One she'd like to know about. "If I give you protection in exchange for a guarantee of security when Yeshua and your people take my city, as I feel they surely will, I'll hide you and cover for you and get you out of here. Now quickly, get up to the roof, where I have much flax drying for making linen, and hide yourselves in case the king's men come looking for you. But first let me show you the way and how the land lies and my plan. Please pay special attention to this. I have a thick, scarlet cord already tied in my window and hanging down the wall outside. I will not be questioned about it, as it is the mark of a woman who does what I do. Please instruct your leaders that it is my sign for security and safety for my household, as I have helped you this day."

Intelligence from behind Enemy Lines

At once the spies felt that they were in safe hands and not being set up for betrayal. "It will be your life for ours, and may Yahweh look upon you with mercy."

To their surprise, Rahav then took a stick and drew a rough plan in the dust of the earthen floor. She showed the river, the Yarden, running north and south and her city, Yeriho, to its west, and further west by south a settlement she called Ay, and she then said, "Now just to the west of the settlement they call Ay is a place our own annals say was once of great significance to your people and to the one you called Ivrahim and his son and his grandson...what was his name? Yaakov?"

Eliav and Nahshon again exchanged knowing glances. This woman was indeed knowledgeable; but, more than that, what they sensed in their deep-in place was awe because settling upon them was the peaceful assurance that Yahweh had led their steps to the right place and the right person at just the right moment.

"And the place west of Ay?" questioned Eliav, with eager anticipation.

"Ah," says Rahav. "It is a series of ridges and plateaus, and it has been called the Mountains of Moriah, and up there is the place known by some as Shalem, to others it's been known as Luz, but to your fathers and your people, it is the place spoken of by your Yaakov, as Bayth-El. Mitsrayim calls it Rushalimum." The men stared at the floor and memorized the picture the extraordinary woman had drawn so that they could reproduce it for Yeshua on their return to the Meadow of the Acacias. In fact, Eliav turned his pouch inside out and tried with a modicum of success to draw the plan onto the leather with a char from Rahav's cooking fire. Between them both, they should be able to give an accurate report.

But Rahav hadn't finished. "I have journeyed a little with my linen and other goods." Her tone was quite confiding

THE PLACE

now that she had a deal with the invaders. "There is another settlement that has occasionally also been called Bayth-el by some because the people of Yevus hold what you call the Bayth-El so firmly. They don't want travelers treating it as a shrine, so they point them north, a half day's walk, to another settlement in the hills of Efrayim. They tell them that's where your Yaakov had his dream. They tell them that's where *the place* is found. So don't be confused." As it turned out, this intelligence was to prove invaluable later, and this is what the plan looked like:

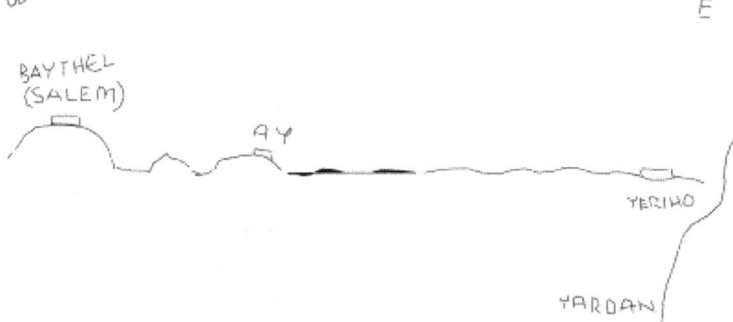

That evening, as the men tried to get a little sleep hidden among great bundles of flax, Nahshon, the more studious of the two, thought deeply about the land they had seen during their reconnaissance. Suddenly, just as Eliav was drifting off into fitful slumber on the hard floor, Nahshon whispered into the blackness. I say he whispered, but in the deathly silence broken only by the tedious but distant *whoo-wu-wu-wooh* of a yanshuph (in our language a great owl), his whisper was a roar.

"Sshh," hissed Eliav.

"Ah-hah, remember how we saw a village half a day to the west by north of here and considered it of not much consequence? That must be the *other* Bayth-el she spoke of. It was in hilly country. Then as we made our way directly south, we realized we were on a major route to the settlement they call Shalem or Yerushalem or...Bayth-El, set on the eastern ridge of one of the hills. It must be the original, the true Bayth-El. It was set high, and we avoided it, but a morning's walk to its east, there was, indeed, a settlement on another ridge. That must be Ay of which Rahav speaks. I remember learning how Father Avram, before he became Ivrahim, came back to the area of Moriah and, after building an altar, moved to the mountain east of Bayth-El and pitched his tent with Bayth-El on the west and Ay on the east.[1] Now it makes sense to me."

---

1. Ref. Gen 12:8

THE PLACE

The yanshuph *whoo-wu'd* in obvious agreement.

Eliav grunted agreement and whispered, "Can we get a bit of sleep now?"

Suddenly Eliav and Nahshon were electrically awake as rough voices were heard below, shattering the stillness, and as the yellow flare of torches made strange shadows leap up the stairs to the roof. The men shrank into the flax, unbreathing, every muscle tight.

And then they heard Rahav's firm and confident voice. "Oh yes, the two men who came to me...you say they were spying out our land? Oh, by the gods, if only I had known... they just had their pleasure and were gone, seemed to be in an awful hurry...barely stopped to pay. They must have rushed out just as the gate was being shut, but it was not long ago. If your men are quick and have lights, you must be able to catch them on the main road." As Nahshon and Eliav heard more shouting followed by the receding clatter of horses' hooves, they breathed again. In no time, Rahav was on the roof, with a length of knotted linen rope tied firmly at one end to the middle of a timber beam. She was strangely composed.

"Come down to the room, and go through the window, and then go further up the mountain, and stay there a few days. Here is bread, and there is plenty of water up there." She threw the rope from the window and down the wall. The beam was wider than the window, so it anchored nicely against the inside of the wall. Her last words to them as they thanked her and slipped, in turn, over the sill to descend into the shadows, was, "Make sure Yeshua knows and sees to our protection."

The men whispered again their promise. "Our life for yours. May Yahweh protect you." They became one with the darkness.

Of course, Yeshua and his people had inklings of what they would encounter. They had had a foretaste to the east of River Yarden, which now stood behind them and which, though in full spate, they had crossed with Yahweh's intervention. In this land were people who sacrificed their firstborn to strange and evil gods, who practiced lewd and licentious acts for their gods and cut or harmed themselves, indulging in all kinds of fear-filled arts to placate these gods. Yahweh had warned them never to adopt or practice such customs, never to be drawn into compromised or syncretistic worship. It is also why Yahweh, over and again, had said to Yeshua, "Be strong and very courageous." It was going to require valor and faith, often the same thing, to both dispossess the evil and occupy its place, filling the void with righteousness.

That was why it came as a body blow when, after triumph at Yeriho, Isra-El was routed and disgraced before the people of the much-smaller Ay. Yeshua knew that it was impossible to occupy without holiness before Yahweh and that the only reason for military failure must have been spiritual failure. One called Akan entitled himself to spoils that Yahweh had instructed were accursed. Akan joined himself to the evil of Kna'an by possessing their goods. After dealing with the failure, Yeshua led his men against Ay again, and here is where our imagined intelligence from Rahav became crucial, as Yahweh gave Yeshua the plan of battle.

As Nahshon had recalled, Father Ivrahim had camped many years before, so the record says, at a mountain east of Bayth-El, having Bayth-El (Shalem) on the west and Ay on the east. As Yeshua made his second attempt on Ay, he sent a party of some five thousand chosen men around to the west by south of Ay by night, and they encamped just south of where Ivrahim had been all those years ago. So with five thousand hidden between Bayth-El and Ay, near dawn, Yeshua led his men to the north of Ay. Between him and the settlement stood a valley and a small, flat plain, and he led his men down into the valley. As soon as the sun was up, the king of Ay assembled his fighting force in the flat area and went after Isra-El. Yeshua led a sham retreat from his position to the north, with the men of Ay pursuing them eastward, as on the previous occasion. Indeed, the men of close neighbor Bayth-El, clearly with a vested interest in seeing off the invaders, joined in the chase. Once they were all drawn away from Ay in pursuit, Yeshua's ambush party, hidden just southward between Ay and Bayth-El, rose and took Ay, burning it. Now the warriors of both Ay and Bayth-El found themselves sandwiched between Yeshua's battalions and were routed, and the city was destroyed.

7

Tzion Is Ours!

> Nevertheless, David took the stronghold of Zion
> (that is, the City of David).
>
> —2 Samuel 5:7 (NKJV)

Many years passed. The walls of the stronghold looked down over Luz, the walled enclosure surrounding that most precious of water supplies, the spring Gikhon, and into the ravine Chedron. To the east, the mount called Khar KhaZeitim, the Mount of Olives, alternated olive groves with gravestones.

A contingent of the best warriors had marched with the thirty-year-old Dawid from Hebron. Their express purpose was to take, finally, the stronghold of Tzion, known as Jevus (after the tribal occupants who had held it inviolate for many years). Dawid knew it to be a key to the purpose of

Yahweh for His people and also sensed that was why it had been a stronghold against the called ones. Called they were, indeed—called to establish right order, called to establish Yahweh's pattern for living, called to exemplify life as *He* intended—and the only way this could be brought to pass was by the dispossession of the terrible evil that inhabited the land. In the eyes of Yahweh, it was to be out with the old and in with the new; out with the unmitigated and unhindered wickedness and immorality that had cursed this land and in with righteousness, shalom, and prosperity for a people who exalted Yahweh. And the place had become a central symbol of defiance against the people of Yahweh who had years before entered this land under one, Yeshua, as the Johnny-come-lately trying to establish a new order and a new god! The Jevusites had territory and land, and saw their central settlement and citadel, Jevus, as the last and final stronghold against such audacity.

Tzion the stronghold was firmly walled, buttressed, and gated against attack, and the proud occupants who had resisted all previous incursions mocked from their lofty citadel the latest colony of ants they saw looking up from the ravine Chedron.

"Even our blind and lame will repel you. You will not get in here," was the mocking cry from the walls.

But the record reveals a "nevertheless." For despite the braggadocio of Yevus, a way was revealed by which one of the strengths of Yevus became its weakness. The fabled spring Gikhon stood just outside and below the main walls of the stronghold on the descent to Chedron. Another fortress wall joining the main city wall had been built out and around the spring, which could be accessed externally or from an internal shaft from the city level. From the stronghold level, vessels could be lowered with ropes to the water and thus filled and drawn up again.

In the soft spring morning light, the walls of the stronghold appeared stark and imposing, even intimidating. The defiant words shouted down from the ramparts of those walls upon Dawid's men were intended to underscore the invincibility of the enclosure, but they were shouted at a man who had heard vaunted invincibility from above him before in the form of a Philistine champion, one Goliat, the Gittite freak. On each occasion, the words of defiance were shouted at a man who was confident in the calling and purpose of Yahweh. Nonetheless, to a lesser man, such words, together with the imposing gray walls towering above the ants in Chedron, could have sufficed to repel any who had not experienced Yahweh as Dawid had.

"My gracious king," intoned Yoav, one of the leading warriors who gazed upward with his king. "How can we proceed?" Yoav was the son of Zeruya, a sister of the king.

"Yoav, my intelligence is that the enclosure jutting eastward from the great wall protects the spring Gikhon at which our fathers drank. It is the place, as you know, where our great one Yaakov had his dream and called it the very Bayth-El. That spring, below and just outside the main wall, has a shaft above it to the city. There is also an external gate to its enclosure. That is where we must take the guard and enter and try to ascend the shaft and take them by surprise."

And then Dawid added to his men, "Whoever leads this attack will be promoted to commander." It was a difficult call, but Yoav led the assault and managed to lead a team in via the shaft, probably under cover of darkness, to eventually take the fortress, Tzion.

It was a most significant moment for Isra-El and, having subjugated the people of Yevus, whose most prominent leader was one Ornan, whose threshing business occupied pride of place near Gikhon, Dawid set about transforming the city. The city now became the City of Dawid, and the king planned and filled[1] and leveled and built and prospered and prepared the way for the building of the Bayth-El: at the place.

---

1. Ref. 2 Sam. 5:9.

8

The Place Changes Hands

> This mountain which His right hand acquired.
> —Psalm 78:54 (NKJV)

> So David gave Ornan six hundred shekels of gold by weight for *the place*.
> —1 Chronicles 21:25
> (NKJV, emphasis added, *ba makom*)

Dawid's Error, God's Redemption

The king was feeling good; it was late spring, and summer, with its promised bounty of grapes, figs, and pomegranates was imminent, and he was on top. His commander in chief had done well in the annual boundary skirmishes and had delivered a wealth of spoil. Moreover, he had delivered the king a new labor force to assist with his construction program. Commander Yoav too had every reason to feel good about himself but was more circumspect and, on this occasion, at least, wiser than his king. The king's brother, a warrior of some note, was also discreet about his fame, even though he had been responsible for dispatching another legendary twelve-fingered, twelve-toed Gittite freak.

The king was feeling so good that he slid into self-congratulation. Something even more insidious than self-satisfaction inveigled its way into his motives and began its display in his attitudes and demeanor. It was even seen in his countenance by those close to him, like Yoav. Call it pride, call it self-importance. Supremacy leads easily to this, and it did with Dawid. His decision to take a census was a reflection of self-importance and self-reliance rather than rest in Yahweh.

As a chilling specter appeared over ancient Yebus and over a specific part of its walled enclave, Ornan had no idea that the flat, rocky slab near Ghikhon Spring on which his oxen threshed wheat and barley had such far-back significance. As he had always done, Ornan and his four sons went through the plodding routine of the threshing. Round and around, the yoke of bored oxen trod as the sons raked trodden grain and chaff aside for winnowing and replaced it with fresh bundles for the circling cloven hooves. The talk was that of farmers and those engaged in crops and agriculture, although Ornan threshed as a business serving local farmers.

"The rains came at the perfect time this year, Father," opined one of the sons.

Ornan's response was to the effect that if they, meaning, of course, the sons, didn't shake themselves up a bit, they'd never keep up and end up losing customers to that shifty operator down in the valley. Ornan had good oxen and a good threshing floor set on the side of a mountain ridge so as to always catch the breezes for winnowing after threshing. The position of his floor meant that the local farmers had to bring their harvest up by cart, but it was worth it for the good, cleanly separated product Ornan and his boys turned out. They were leaders in their trade and Ornan a prominent and influential citizen; the family business was secure.

Life was pretty good in Yevus, and they were happy enough about the new king who had, not too long back, taken Yevus and wanted a new name for it; the name *Yevus*, as chief city of the Yevusites, a diminished clan of Kna'an, didn't sit well with the new conquerors. It meant "downtreader" or "to tread underfoot," and the new king's God, known as Yahweh, or El Elyon, or Adonai, frequently renamed and gave new meaning to those things of which He took possession or repossession. Thus, Avram had become Ivrahim and Sarai Sarah; Yaakov the Supplanter had been transformed to Isra-el, "prevailing with God." Now

Yevus was to become City of Dawid and later Yerushalem, "foundation of peace."

But as we said, apart perhaps from a small irritation over the renaming plan, all was good for Ornan and his family—until now!

Of course, Ornan had heard the stories of the God of Isra-El, and there were many things about the religious practices of some of his own Yevusites and other people of Kna'an that had disturbed him, like the idea of offering children to Moloch in the fire; the orgiastic "worship" among the prostitutes provided for the purpose; and the bestiality, drunkenness, and gluttony of the festivals, not to mention the prostitution and willful using of children for sexual perversion. Yahweh had been careful to ensure that these peoples who had so corrupted and polluted the land knew that there was a better way to live. Disappointed as Yahweh was at the almost universal decline into independence, self-will, and corruption since the warnings and purging and eventual restart with Noe and then the next decline to Bavel, *He* desired a "demonstration" people among the Goyim. This would at least leave them without excuse. If who *He* was, what He expected, and what He could do for a people was clearly evident, people groups would have a clear choice—a choice between His favor and the independence, which always seemed to result in the dreaded hollowness. The choice would be theirs, and therefore, the outcome would be a chosen outcome.

THE PLACE

The Goyim—those other nations—all knew about the outstanding defeat of the pantheon of Mitsrayim (or Egypt, as we call it) and Isra-El's emancipation from there; they all knew of the miraculous events that accompanied this unique people. Information traveled up and down the trade routes quite quickly, and the exploits of the God called Elohim and Yahweh and Adonai had such eyewitness veracity that its effect was to strike awe and inquiry into the peoples—as Yahweh intended. They heard too of Yahweh's exclusive demands and the lifestyle He desired. "No other gods beside me!" No other gods? That would require a full change of disposition; an abandoning of a pantheon of invented deities they'd known from childhood and an abandoning of practices they'd come to loathe whilst still loving and by which they had been enslaved. Their gods truly held them in thrall, and so few sought to choose *Him* and to side with Isra-El's God.

That Yahweh's plan to show the way among the peoples was often effective is evident, but, as in all ages, people were reluctant to admit to truth that stared them in the face for fear they may have to relinquish cherished autonomy.

Ornan represented the stranglehold the Yevusites had on the place. What was clearly of importance to Yahweh and His relationship with the people He had chosen as His representatives was also, therefore, of great interest to the enemies of Yahweh. Possession of the place implied the superiority of Yevusite and Kna'anite gods. It made a statement. Even Yeshua the Courageous, with his committed people, had failed to dislodge them by becoming occupants of the citadel wherein the place stood. After the death of Yeshua, the children of Yudah and of Benyamin fought against Yevus and took it, but they also failed to occupy. The command of Yahweh had been to dislodge Yevusites (and others) by occupying what they had once occupied. Occupation was the command that had not been properly or fully implemented. The word *yaresh*, in the command of Yahweh, means "to occupy by dispossession of other occupants." There is no partial occupation; it is a contradiction.

(Did not the Great One who came so much later speak a similar truth when He said, "When an unclean spirit goes out of a man, he goes through dry places seeking rest, and finding none, he says, 'I will return to the house from which I came.' And finding it swept and in order, he goes and finds seven other spirits more wicked than himself, and they enter and occupy the house." The cleaned house cannot be left vacant.)

As we said, life had been good for Ornan—until now!

All saw the angelic specter above them and responded in markedly different ways. The sons scurried into hiding. Ornan, perhaps hoping what he just had seen would not be there when next he looked, turned back to the task at hand. When next and tentatively he looked up to the clatter of shod horses, who should be standing in front of him but

THE PLACE

Dawid, the king, easily recognizable in kingly attire and with a retinue of guards and officials. Now he knew not which perplexed him more, the presence of the specter or the presence of the king! Ornan stumbled out from the threshing floor and bowed low.

The king was urgent. "Ornan, you must sell me the place of your threshing floor at full price, as I've been commanded to make here an altar to the Lord, Yahweh."

Now a tangled matrix of thoughts competed within Ornan's startled mind for supremacy. A moment ago he and his sons had been doing what they did so frequently and so well; the humdrum that was so filled with smells of field and grain and straw and leather and sweat and manure and sounds of squabbling birds. Then all of that seemed suspended momentarily—the *plod, plod, plod* of hooves, the creak of equipment, the shuffling of Ornan's sandals—for the oxen had propped as the specter's presence unnerved and balked them. And then they reluctantly resumed as Ornan spoke reassurance to them and tried valiantly to pretend all was well. The birds left a cloud of wheat dust and a thrum of wing beat hanging in the still air as they propelled themselves all in opposite, panicked directions.

Word had crept out and about from the king's court that Dawid and his commander in chief had been at odds over the king's insistence on a census of his military strength. The king's word had prevailed against Yoav, who had reluctantly obeyed, but as a token of his disgust counted all but the tribes of Levi and Benyamin. The king had in all of Isra-El one million and one hundred thousand men who drew the sword and in Yudah 470 thousand; but in desiring the count, Dawid showed that, unlike his forefather Ivrahim, he had not yet passed the test of utter dependence. The consequences were dire and stretched beyond the throne. Dawid's failure affected the realm with a plague even though the king had asked Yahweh to spare the people and afflict him only.

"Take it and the oxen as sacrifice and the implements as firewood and the wheat as a grain offering. I'll gladly give it all." The image of the specter was still imprinted somewhere behind Ornan's eyes.

"No, for I cannot offer to Yahweh that which cost me nothing." With that, a transaction was effected and recorded, and legal title to the far-back place, *the place*, passed to the House of Dawid (and remains there to this day). The record states, "So Dawid gave Ornan six hundred shekels of gold by weight for *the place*[1]." The king built the altar and sacrificed and called on Yahweh, who answered by fire there. The specter, in the form of an angel with sword drawn for punishment, withdrew. The plague halted. In seeking aggrandizement, Dawid had been instead diminished by seventy thousand men, and the king said, in words now familiar to us, the words of Yaakov of old: "This

---

1.   1 Chron. 21:25 NKJV emphasis added (*ba makom*)

is the Bayth-El,[2] and this is the altar of burnt offering for Isra-El."

And so Dawid began preparation for the house. *The place* had been of no account in the eyes of the citizens of Yevus, whose name means "downtreader," just a good place for a threshing floor, a place to be trodden underfoot by men and oxen. Its far-back significance meant nothing to them except as a good water source. To these Kna'anites, worshipers of idols, sacrificers of children, bound by superstitions and fears, what could a rocky outcrop on the side of a hill near Ghikhon, where "they" said a god had had dealings with their ancestors, mean?

Dawid the warrior-king was not destined to build the Bayth-El. That privilege fell to his son, Shalomoh, whose name meant "man of peace." It was he, Shalomoh, who later prayed at the spectacular dedication of the great Bayth-El, "That Your eyes may be open toward this temple night and day, toward *the place* of which you said 'My name shall be there[3].'"

---

2.   1 Chron. 22:1. Author's freehand translation: David said Bayth-Yahweh-El, "this the house of the Lord God", adding Yahweh in the name.

3.   1 Kings 8:29 and refer also to 2 Chronicles 7:12–15 NKJV emphasis added (*ha makom and ba makom*).

9

The Tent at Ghikhon

And he (Dawid) prepared a place for the ark of God and pitched *a tent* for it.

—1 Chronicles 15:1
(NKJV, parenthesis added, emphasis added)

And have Solomon my son ride on my own mule and take him down to *Gikhon*.

—1 Kings 1:33 (NKJV, emphasis added)

So Zadok the priest, Nathan the prophet...went down and had Solomon ride on king Dawid's mule, and took him to *Gikhon*. Then Zadok the priest took a horn of oil *from the tent* and anointed Solomon.

—1 Kings 1:38–39 (NKJV, emphasis added)

"Ah," said Priest Zadok one day to Nathan and the old King Dawid. "For too long the tent of Moshe has stood at Gibeon. It has awaited the day when Yerushalem was ours, and it can be superseded by the structure Yahweh has put in the king's heart."

"How well I remember the day when you, Nathan, brought the word of Yahweh to me that it would be my son Shalomoh and not me who would build the Bayth-El. Oh, but in His grace and by His Spirit, He has given me the plans that I might see it with the mind's eye. By faith I have enjoyed their preparation and the preparation of the materials and the gold and silver, but I am so glad that at least I was able to make a tent for the ark and pitch it at Ghikhon—at *the place*—and that we were able to anoint my son Shalomoh there! My tent has stood there at Ghikhon these twenty and seven years as a kind of marker and faith builder for the Bayth-El that he will build on that dedicated spot. That is why I have written of the temple *He* has put in my heart as though it exists! My dear Nathan, have the scribe read me the song that speaks about the oracle in my heart and His love reaching to the heavens, for in that, I believe, I spoke about the fountain and the stream that is right there with Him wherever He resides."

The scribes hastened to the parchments, and soon one stood by the king's bed, reading: "How precious your lovingkindness, O God! Therefore the children of men put their trust under the shadow of Your wings. They are abundantly satisfied with the fullness of Your house, and

You give them drink from the river of Your pleasures, for with You is the fountain of life."[5]

The king, old now, somewhat sad-eyed and reclining in his bed, brightened and spoke slowly and deliberately. "Ah yes, that's the one I had in mind. You see, my loyal friends, His wings that cover and protect us are represented there by those of the cherubim above the mercy seat, and there too, at the place, Gikhon represents His life-giving fountain and the stream of His pleasures from which we may always drink! In the sense that *He* has shown me all this, I too have participated in the greater house to come, then the old tent of Moshe that has stood at Gibeon, the one that represents transience and sojourning, can be taken down. Blessed be the name of Yahweh!" He sighed because even collecting his thoughts and speaking had now become wearisome. His physicians brought a brazier closer for warmth, and his advisors indicated to Nathan and Zadok that they should bring their appointment to an end.

They took their leave of the king and departed to the soft sounds of Dawid's own harp being played by one of his favorite musicians.

Nathan too remembered the day when he had said to Dawid, "Do all that is your heart, for Yahweh is with you." Then how difficult he had found it to return the next day with what Yahweh had said overnight—that it would be Shalomoh, not Dawid, who would build the Bayth-El!

---

5 Psalm 36:7–9 NKJV

10

Darkness

Bayth-El or Bayth-el?

The belly of the monstrous bronze beast, with its gaping maw open and sloping back and up from the plinth on which it sat, was a furnace ablaze with pine fire. The beast itself had a huge bovine head above the yawning maw, and human arms and hands. It sat on its stone plinth, as we said, its leering head gazing lifelessly out over the living who genuflected and fawned ridiculously before it. Seated on its haunches, the arms and hands were outstretched to the front so that the flames, once the inferno was well alight, swept upward around them to engulf whatever had been placed in them by the frenzied, shrieking, dancing priests and priestesses. The scene was devilish, depraved, repugnant. Among the awful smells were those of human flesh burning. Worse, the flesh was that of human babes.

"Aba, who is Molech?" the young child's face was covered with perplexity. Her parents froze. If the first question made them freeze, her second caused a prayer to be instantly dispatched heavenward: "Dear Yahweh, save!" for her second question was, "Mother, what happened to my friend Ephrath's new little brother?" It was clear that their precious and innocent daughter was making a connection they had hoped she would not at her tender age of seven. A drop of sweat appeared on the father's brow, and hard-to-disguise tears pooled quickly in her mother's eyes to overflow down her flushed cheeks. Troubled glances were exchanged, and then the father spoke.

Wisely, Ariel talked to her of Yahweh's mercy and *chesed*[1] commitment to His special people and His promises to them and of His nature and of their very own experience of His provision for them. In turn, Ariel and the child's mother, Diana, took her in their arms and spoke of Father Ivrahim and of Yitzchaq and of Yaakov, and of Moshe and Yeshua, and of Keleb, of Shemuel, Elishu'a and Eliyyahu, until the little girl said her head was not keeping up!

"Dawid," Ariel said, "was our great king, used by Yahweh to unite Isra-El and Yudah. His son Shalomoh after him built up the great Bayth-El we hope you will one day see in Yerushalem, with Yahweh's will, His great name be praised.

---

1. The Hebrew word *chesed* means relentless covenant loyalty and faithfulness.

THE PLACE

It was then known as the City of Dawid. Ah, we remember the last of those days. You know, sweet one, we used to go up there to the festivals and worship and praise and hear the word of Yahweh and..." Ariel trailed off into distant reverie, his voice now disconnecting from its source. He struggled to bring himself back from the joys embedded within the memories. "Little one, all you need to know is that not all sons follow in their father's steps. We have now a king who is not like Dawid. Even the great Shalomoh, as wise as he had been, became led astray and at the end built shrines for many of the gods of his foreign wives—yes, even that ghastly Molech you asked about. Then it is said that King Yerovom divided the kingdom and followed the ways of the deceived peoples that Yahweh had helped us clean out of much of the land. Sadly, we failed to completely dispossess them and to fully occupy our land; peoples, would you believe, dear child, who make gods invented from their own minds and whom they imagine require terrible things of them? The land was polluted by their evil and horrid acts—I cannot speak of them—and that is why Yahweh had instructed His people to dispossess them. But alas, we, the people of Yahweh, are in danger of being no better."

Then Ariel brightened. "We pray for the fulfillment of the prediction of that man of God from Yudah who challenged that evil Yerovom![2] He cried against the high

---

2. See I Kings 13:1 & 2

place that Yerovom had set up, in the other Bayth-el and, would you believe, there were even false altars set up right in the true Bayth-El itself, and the man of God said a king would come by the name of Yosiayuh, who is to tear them down and lead us back to Yahweh, praised be His powerful name!"

The bright child, Penina (their Pearl) was ahead of them in wits and sometimes in faith. "O Father, how could grown-ups believe and do what they think a god like that tells them? I saw a carving of it at Ephrath's, and it's made up. She told me her family is afraid of it, and she told me scary things about it. I know what happened to Ephrath's brother. It was given to that…that…thing, wasn't it, Mother? Wasn't it, Father?" She was surprisingly calm and assured and disarming, but then she wept into the comforting arms of her parents for a long time. After it was over, she said, "I'm glad Yahweh is our real God, with real prophets and real priests and real words and…and real miracles.

"I love it when Uncle Venyamin talks to me about the great prophets and Yahweh's law and about how Yahweh has let him know how real He is when he prays and when he worships. He told me about Yerushalem too. O Father, I so want to go there with you, but Uncle Venyamin must be confused because he sometimes calls Yerushalem Bayth-El!" She was smiling again now, and her parents said it was the smile of faith. And then this: "What shall I say to Ephrath?"

Ariel and Diana said, "Let's ask Yahweh, and He will help you to know what to say. Say nothing unless Ephrath talks about it and then just love her like you know Yahweh loves her...and you...and then you can tell her you don't want to follow a god who is like that. You want to follow Yahweh. But don't be drawn into a fight about it!"

But there were more questions. "But, Father, I am confused. Tell me about Bayth-El. Why does Uncle Venyamin call it Bayth-El? Is that not another place?"

"Ah," said Ariel kindly. "I understand your confusion. Let me try to explain as simply as I can." He gathered his thoughts for a moment as Diana, more assured now, offered water and raisin cakes for Penina and some rose-colored wine with nuts and dates she had fetched from the markets that morning for her husband. The tenth hour of the day was a good time for refreshments, especially when it meant some meaningful time with Ariel's beloved Pearl.

"You see, my daughter, there is a true Bayth-El, right within the boundaries of Dawid's City. Our great prophet Yeshaayah has called it the Bayth-El of Yaakov.[3] And then there's another village not far away, up in the hills of Efrayim, almost as high up as Yerushalem and to the north, that became a kind of counterfeit."

---

3. Isaiah 2:3 and also Micah 4:2 both of which say, "the Bayth-El of Yaakov" see eg., Scripture4 All interlinear Bible. The Bayth-El of Yaakov was on the mountain of the Lord!

"A what?"

"A kind of pretend. You remember the stories of our father Yaakov...and indeed even before him, the great Ivrahim? They were led to what became known to our people as *the place*. It's where Ivrahim met Yahweh as Yireh and where Yaakov had his amazing dream and made a promise to *Him* and called *the place* Bayth-El. He believed it to be very special, where the great El Elohim or Yahweh or El Shaddai or Adonai—we call Him all these wonderful names because they are what *He* is like—where *He* was putting His presence as nowhere else." His tone showed he was warming to his subject and to the imparting opportunity. The security written on Penina's face said all she needed to say.

Diana had been half listening, and she broke in. "But why have two places so close together with the same name? It *is* very confusing."

"Agreed, but it is my understanding that because the stronghold of Yevus and its ever-flowing spring, Gikhon, was so impregnable and defended so aggressively until our Dawid took it, there was no access to *the place* for pilgrims or wayfarers or indeed anyone. So as these things do, the nearest convenient place where there was a spring, just a half day's walk to the north, took on the identity, and the name stuck."

"Near enough was good enough?"

"Sort of," responded Ariel.

THE PLACE

"I can see how that could eventuate," mused Diana. Penina was drifting into that faraway land where her parents' words and voices were now a distant background sound to her own imaginings and thought games.

Ariel continued, "Pilgrims and travelers could get close and view the true Bayth-El from the hills opposite, across the valley Chedron, but the spring Gikhon and the city Yevus above were so fortified and guarded that no outsider was allowed to come near. You see, the city and its walls and battlements were on a neck or peninsula leading south from Moriah. Some called it Luz, after the name of a neck bone, I suppose because that's what it reminded them of.

That neck or ridge has deep valleys east, south, and west, making it easy to defend and almost impregnable. Remember, water is our most precious resource."

"So," Ariel continued with affection for them both, and around a mouthful of date. "That special place, Bayth-El, is indeed a portion within our great city, the City of Dawid. It is just up from Chedron and beneath and just to the east of Shalomoh's temple. The spring has a fortress wall around it. It's where those great men stood and where our great King Dawid stood and purchased *the place* from the Yevusite, Ornan, who had his threshing floor there. But the real Bayth-El is even more. We have told you of Gan Edhen?

"This is where that garden once was before the great deluge and the ark of Noe, and where *He* walked with the first one made, the first one of us, whose name was 'Dam."

Ariel gave Penina a little nudge, for this, he felt, was important. "So the settlement that began as Shalem became known over the years as Luz, Bayth-El, Yevus, and then Yerushalem, and then more lately as the City of Dawid, Tzion, or the mountain of Yahweh—it has so many names! But it is at its heart Bayth-El, where *He* lives! That's why the greatest of our kings, Shalomoh, whose name, by the way, also comes from *shalom*, built the great house of worship—the great Bayth-El—right there on the special spot!"

"Shamah!" shrieked the excited young girl with delight. "I've heard it's got lots of gold and beautiful stones and about the twelve lions and..."

"Yes, all of that and more," Ariel broke into her breathlessness. "All that and more. But most important is not the building but Who it points to in the special way that it's built and how it leads into the Holy Place and the Most Holy Place, where the tablets are in the ark and..." Now Ariel was getting breathless as memories came flooding back.

There was too much to tell at once, and he called himself back to his purpose. "Yes, the other Bayth-el, it is just a half day's walk north of the true Bayth-El. It suited perfectly that tricky king Yerovom, who split our kingdom, to turn it into a shrine to the gods of the Ammonites and other peoples. It was right on the highway into Yerushalem from the north so that pilgrims coming up to the true Bayth-El could be seduced by Yerovom before they came to *the place*.

Yerovom told people from the north they didn't have to go into Yerushalem to make offering. Here was a Bayth-el with priests and gods and everything they needed for their wellbeing! But his big statement was the gold calves that he put in his Bayth-el. He said they were the gods who brought us out of Mitsrayim!"

At times he used vocabulary that young Penina did not quite understand, but she understood the idea.

Ariel reclined on the comfortable cushions. He was a thin man, and his bony left arm and hip needed accommodating support for the serious right-handed business of dates and nuts and wine. He looked around at his ample home and his attractive wife and his Pearl, and a flush of thankfulness wafted over him.

Though he still hoped and prayed for a son, he and his daughter had a special bond. He was a potter with a good kiln and a better reputation that brought custom from near and far. His sign on an urn was said to be worth an extra half shekel, even one, and his town had plenty of well-to-do folk who appreciated quality. Further, Ariel was a godly man known for his integrity and wisdom. Although only forty and five years, he had more than once been invited to come and sit in their city gate to assist with a difficult adjudication.

To Penina, he added, as a further thought struck him, "It is because there are really two Bayth-els—the original and the pretend—that our scribes have sometimes distinguished between them with a description, my dearest Penina. For example, in the times of the judges we've talked to you about, the beloved D'vorah, it was recorded, used to sit under a tree that became known as her palm tree. It was described as being between Ramah and the Bayth-el that is in the hill country of Efrayim."[4]

Penina was becoming restless, and perhaps the explanation was more than she had asked for. "Aba, please talk to me more about Yahweh. I love Him and love to hear about Him. When I hear about Him, I think I'm starting to know Him because...it makes something happen in here." She moved her hand over her chest and smiled contentedly, and then she played with her dark tresses and a bone hairpin that was her mother's. Next thing she was asleep, and the next thing after that, so was Ariel.

Diana said, "Yahweh, I praise you," and busied herself with unnecessary little tasks.

When they both stirred again, Ariel had another disconnected thought that he felt obliged to add to the overload: "Remember how our great king Dawid slew the giant from Gath and brought the giant's huge, hairy head back to the camp with him? Later, when Yerushalem became truly ours and truly occupied by us, Dawid put Goliat's head in Yerushalem, and he kept the giant's armor too! It was such an icon of Dawid's and Yahweh's victory. It's said

---

4. Judges 4:5

that there's a place where it was finally buried, perhaps with King Dawid, and it's also said that people took to calling the place where it was buried Golgotha[5] because Goliat of Gath's head was there! And the name stuck!"

But Penina had already begun to wander off and take an interest in what her mother was doing as she cleaned, in readiness for the evening walk to the well, a water vessel that was the envy of other women because Ariel had fashioned it and decorated it for her.

"Mother, can I come with you today…please? Ephrath's mother lets her go with her."

Ariel chuckled around another mouthful of dates and nuts. "He'ach!," he muttered to no one particular. "Maybe Goliat's head represents all of Yahweh's enemies that are to be crushed when He of whom the prophets speak comes." He thought this was a clever inspiration, but it was lost in the warm afternoon air, the activity and chatter of mother and daughter, not to mention the gently soporific effect of the wine.

---

5. In the reader's language, "Skull Place."

11

I Am Yosiayuh

LORD, I have loved the habitation of your house and *the place* where your glory dwells.
—Psalm 26:8 (NKJV, emphasis added, *u makom*)

I have reigned in Yerushalem—or, as some call it, Bayth-El, and others Tzion or Dawid's city or even Luz—for some twenty-seven years now. I was but eight years old when I came to the throne, and but for my childhood grooming from sound and godly advisors (and certainly not from my father, who, fortunately, had little input to my formation), things might have been very different; I may have been like my grandfather Menashe and my father, Awmon. Astonishingly, my arrival was foretold more than three hundred years ago by a man of God, the prophet from

Yudah, when that mordant king Yerovom was working his evil heart's desire throughout the land.

I praise and glorify Yahweh for what he has enabled me to achieve thus far, for when Hilkyah the priest rediscovered the book of the law of Yahweh, and Shaphan, my scribe and trusted servant, began to read it to me, I was smitten. Smitten because I could immediately see how far we, the people of Yahweh, had drifted from Him and His heart's desire.

> Dear Scribe Shaphan,
> Let the record show what you already know; that I forthwith sought Yahweh with my whole heart. Let it show that Hilkiyah and Ahiykam and Aachbor and the good prophet Yerimyeh and you yourself have assisted me greatly in this endeavor— Oh yes, and the prophetess Chuldah who assured me from Yahweh that I would not see the calamity *He* would bring on *the place*..[1]

Shaphan bowed deeply even though he had lived at the king's elbow, as it were, these many years. He was an aging man now, with a white and wavy beard. The pen knife he had used all these years hung on a thong from his girdle, and he gave it a quick hone on a river stone kept in a pocket of his vestment for the purpose. Nimble fingers sharpened

---

1. 2 Kings 22:20 (*ha makom*).

again, more from habit than necessity, one of his thin reed pens with the same well-worn and beloved knife. Shaphan loved what he did. He felt it was his calling, and he loved Yahweh and delighted in the sense of purpose he knew within, as he recorded the business of the court and the house Bayth-El and the nation. He had witnessed with joy the cleaning out of the foul images of Ba'al and Aserah and other detritus, as he liked to call it, from the temple, right there in Bayth-El, Yerushalem!

"Remember, Shaphan, how you were with me when I set about destroying all those corrupt Ba'al and Aserah images and worship around Yerushalem, even within the true Bayth-El, and in the high places? We burned them all outside Yerushalem and carried the ashes to the counterfeit Bayth-el[2] that King Yerovom had built in the hill country of Ephraim."

"Oh yes," responded Shaphan. "And I well remember that we carried all that detritus there as a sign that that was where it belonged and not in the true Bayth-El, and how the hand of Yahweh was with us because we had control over Shomaron again since the days when our good king Abaiyah had prevailed against Yerovom,[3] praise be to Yahweh!"

---

2. 2 Kings 23:4.
3. 2 Chron. 13:19.

"It was there at Bayth-el in Shomaron that I discovered the tomb of the prophet from Yudah who had actually foretold my arrival and actions so long before.[4] Finding that was a real confirmation from Yahweh Himself and gave me great assurance and blessing and confidence in Him."

And so the king and his closest friend and confidant reflected, and Shaphan set the facts in writing.

---

4. 2 Kings 23:16–18.

12

Homeward Bound!

> But if you return to Me, and keep My commandments and do them, though some of you were cast out to the farthest part of the heavens, yet I will gather them from there, and bring them to *the place* which I have chosen as a dwelling for my name
>
> —Nehemiah 1:9
> (NKJV, emphasis added, *ha makom*)

There are some who remember, just a few. They are old now, so old, and they speak of the place with faraway hearts and voices. They call it Yerushalem, Bayth-El, Tzion, the City of Dawid, or the mountain of the Lord, with a connection and a yearning that wells up from their deep place. Some just call it *the place*. The young, being born here in Bavel, know nothing of it but what they hear from the aged, but in their hearts too, it has assumed legendary status. Bavel (or Babylon, as the reader knows it) is majestic, an astonishment to the world, with its vast walls, plazas, gardens and waterways, the man-made mountain, and that extraordinary inner gate to the honor of Ishtar (she who would bring fertility), the gate leading to the processional way through the city center! Oh, it is indeed majestic. But to us, even those who've never seen the homeland, it offers no comparison to our legendary city.

We have been told that the kings of the world came to behold what our Shalomoh built—the Bayth-El and his own house, the chariots and the horses and stables—all of great splendor that brought fame to our Yahweh. We've been told that gold was as common as iron in that city. Can it be?

But we know too from the aged, who prefer to speak more of the splendor than of the shame, that even Shalomoh went astray, as did most who followed him on the throne. And that is why we are here, as the great Yahweh told. Is there a God like Him, who speaks with His mouth and can fulfil with His hand? We have seen the gods of this land, and they are vain. Men expend great energy and enterprise to fashion their imagined likeness! Praise be to Yahweh that even here, some of our champions have caused the kings of this place to acknowledge *Him* as the One!

"The news, the news! Praise Yahweh!" shouted the staggering old man. "The proclamation in the square!

Kurosh has decreed the restoration of Yerushalem and our temple!" He was shaking and wanted to say more but could not, for the words could neither be found nor formed. People rushed to Hatipha's aid and gained from him, once he was seated and had taken some water, that he had just now come from the city center, the public square where the king's scribes had made a proclamation.

Parosh, one of the first to the old man's aid, and something of a leader, looked quickly at a young man and said, "Run, Giddel, and see what this is about. Take the route by the weaver's street and come back quickly."

Hatipha was among the aged who remembered from youth the grandeur, the intrinsic unity, and very rightness, as he liked to call it, of home. Yes, memories were tinctured and photo-touched by time and distance and many retellings, but nevertheless true and a true expression of what was in many a heart in Bavel. Parosh knew the old man well and spoke kindness to him as he fanned him and made him comfortable.

"I don't doubt you, dear Hatipha, but I've sent younger legs to get more information. The changes since King Kurosh took Bavel are amazing. The Persian acts with the greatest of respect toward us. Mind you, I believe Nebukadnetstsar generally treated us well too."

"It is so," interrupted Hatipha, returning to the reverie that most had heard often from his lips, "Do you know that he, Nebukadnetstsar, worshipped and gave praise to Yahweh after the miraculous deliverance of our great Daniel? And do you know of the visions of Daniel and, and, and...what of the prophetic word of our great seer Yeremeyeh? It is coming to pass. It is coming to pass in the seventy years he foretold! He said that *He* would fulfill his promise and bring us back to the place!"[1]

Somewhat to the relief of Parosh, not because he was rude but because every time he saw Hatipha, he heard his stories, Giddel came panting back to the clutch of Jews gathered to Hatipha's welfare.

"It is true, and the king himself is to make a public appearance in two days to put his seal on the proclamation and put the parchment up in the square. It's going to be like a festival with prominent men of the Hebrew nation present to receive a copy of the proclamation." He paused while he caught his breath. "Kurosh has even asked for harps and some of our songs of Tzion. Now we'll be able to sing them!"

Giddel too, even though he'd never been to Tzion, was getting excited and began an impromptu dance right there, linking arms with the nearest of the group and whirling in a circle, shouting hallelujah. Even old Hatipha was now on

---

1. Jer. 29:10 NKJV and Scripture4All interlinear (*ha makom*). Note: Jeremiah uses *ha makom* many times (e.g., 16:9; 19:3; 24:5; 27:22; 28:3, 4, 6; 32:37; 40:2; 42:18. In all of these it is, "this, *the place*" emphasis added).

THE PLACE

his feet and joining in until there was such a cloud of dust and noise and sweat and gathering crowd that mounted guards came up, all of a clatter, brandishing arms and calling for quiet! Needless to say, the excitement swept through the Hebrew community, and that night was a long one of rejoicing and visiting with each other and sharing food and wine and of remembering the words of their great prophet Yeremeyeh about the seventy years.

Hatipha spent the evening rejoicing with the wife of his youth, who, from their meager means and family and friends, prepared a meal of game and field vegetables and of bread and raisin cakes. She, Daaliah, was a woman of great charm and character, having stood with her husband all these years in an alien and difficult land. She had determined to honor Yahweh, and that determination had many times made life hard in this place. Her face, though full of grace and sweetness, nonetheless now carried the lines of age and a certain weariness. The talk with friends and family was already about how a return would ever be accomplished and, indeed, whether Daaliah and Hatipha were up to the very long journey.

They need not concern themselves, for there were exceedingly capable men just for the times; and after the day of celebration and the king's pomp and the homeland music and the dances, which all the people of Bavel applauded, the one, Zrubbavel, took the lead. But the king's decree! Oh, it was the real music of the day. The music of the harps and the pipes and timbrels was made the richer by what the king read, for here it is:

> Yahweh, the God of heaven, has given me all the kingdoms of the earth, and He has appointed me to build a temple for Him at Yerushalem in Yudah. Anyone of His people among you—may his God be with him and let him go up to Yerushalem in Yudah and build the Bayth-El of Yahweh, the God of Isra-El, the God who is in Yerushalem.[2]

At this point, the king had to pause. Such was the upwelling of emotion and hallelujahing and shouts of joy that even he became overcome and had to quickly take wine and compose himself. For, although a man of great self-importance, speaking words of pomp, there crept over him a sense that what he had just spoken was actual.

It was not the usual kowtowing to the god who happened to be de rigueur or whom his counselors said it would be politically expedient to give attention to.

He had never sensed this before; perhaps these people really were under a greater Hand than his.

He intoned in his best enlightened and self-congratulatory tones, "Let the Bayth-El at Yerushalem

---

2. Ezra 1:2-4 Author's paraphrase. Note Ezra 5:13 "to build this Bayth-El" and 6:3 "the Bayth-El *at* Yerushalem" Emphasis added.

be rebuilt, the place where they offered sacrifices,"[3] and it went on and on, with instructions for its foundations and its expanse and the finances and the people in charge and the provisions for the offerings, and oh, it was a decree that made the old ones weep and the young ones cheer! And it settled upon all the Hebrews in that place, young and old, how the words of their Yahweh, once spoken with His mouth, would always be fulfilled with His hand.

The citizens of Bavel had not seen a day like it, for cheer and goodwill and spontaneity and song to Yahweh, and dance, without the drunkenness or debauchery (not to mention the ensuing regret and ill will) of their own feasts; and they could not help but compare. There were even some who desired to come with them on their adventure!

The one, Zrubbavel, had been born here in Bavel, as his name said, but had grown up under godly tutelage that kept him from the errant ways of his grandfather Yehoyakin, the very last king of homeland Yudah before the deportation. And with him was to be Yeshua as high priest and Nechemyah and Mordekay and Bigshaan; oh, and so many of the distinguished ones—men of skill and wisdom. Kurosh decreed that all that was needed should be supplied, and the plan proceeded quickly and efficiently under these great men.

---

3. Ezra 6:3 ff Author's paraphrase

"Praise to the name of Yahweh Almighty!" Hatipha was newly energized, and there was a spark in his eyes as he talked with Daaliah. "We are going in caravan with escort from the king and with all the food and comforts we need for the journey," he explained to her.

She had made herself up with lotions and aloes and perfumes, and her dark, dark eyes reflected the yellow flame of the oil lamp that stood between them on a small pedestal as they reclined after dining. The room was so still that the flame of the lamp flickered only when one of them spoke. In its light, he saw again the beauty of the young virgin he had taken to himself in the homeland just over seventy years ago, and a tear teased the corner of one eye before running all the way down the channel between his nose and his cheek, across his lips to salt his tongue. The tear from the other eye fell to the cushion. He leaned over to kiss her on the lips and tasted also the salt of her tears. They both felt young again, for they had been chosen to go as being among the few who could remember how things once were at Bayth-El.

13

I Am Zekharayah

To beautify *the place* of my sanctuary; and I will make *the place* of my feet glorious.

—Isaiah 60:13
(NKJV, emphasis added, *u makom*)

And in *the place* I will give peace.

—Haggai 2:9 (*u ba makom*)

Many peoples will come and say, "Come, let us go up to the mountain of the lord, to the *bayth-El of Yaakov*. He will teach us His ways; for out of Tzion goes forth Torah, and the word of the lord from Yerushalem."

—Isaiah 2:3 and Micah 4:2

IAN HEARD

Yes, I am Zekharayah, and here I am in the place! My parents taught me of it, and my grandfather too, the one, Iddo the seer, respected among my people for his wisdom and prophetic gift. Here I am, and I have found that Yahweh has also given me words, which I must speak, though I am of Levi. But why should I not be both priest and prophet? It is *He* who has so ordained; I shall not question, for I would please Him as did my grandfather and my father. I was born in Bavel during the duress, as was my compatriot Zrubbavel, whose name means "offspring of Bavel" and who has been made governor in Yudah by that most enlightened of kings of Persia, now controlling Bavel, the one, Kurosh. My name means, to you who read, "Yahweh remembers," and oh, how it delights me now to realize the prescient nature of the name pronounced over me by my father those thirty-some years ago!

Yerushalem is in a ruined state, but Kurosh has sent us (he says by our Lord Yahweh!) to reestablish our religion and culture. Indeed, our own great seer Yeshaayah has, I believe, called him, that is, Kurosh—"Yahweh's anointed"! There is also our beloved prophet Khaggay bringing a message to encourage the completion of the temple. Thanks be to Yahweh for the words of Khaggay! May Yahweh give him shalom!

Oh, and while I think of prophet Yeshaayah, Yahweh has also given *me* a picture of rivers of living waters flowing

THE PLACE

out from Yerushalem.¹ Just as streams used to flow from Gan Edhen right here, so new streams of life will one day flow from here; yes, from Bayth-El in Yerushalem, from the place! The spring Ghikhon is a picture of living water at Tzion, or the Bayth-El of Yaakov, as Yeshaayah called it; there must be living water at the Bayth-El! The Bayth-El is a source, our source! But long ago, our people began to despise it and esteem it lightly. Did not Yeshaayah say, "Because this people esteems lightly the water of Shiloah (Ghikhon) that flows with gentleness, the Lord will bring over them the waters of the River (Euphrates)"²

Interestingly, speaking of Bayth-El, this very day I had to answer questions of our own people; they sent two representatives to come to me here in Bayth-El (I have insisted that my scribe use the true name of the place in the recording, for they came here to the priests to entreat Yahweh)³ and I had to answer with words that came from Yahweh. The spokesmen were Sherezer and Regem-Melech, who desired to know about the fasts in memory of the destruction of the temple so long ago. It was, I think, a diversion because there has been a certain lack of

---

1. Zech. 14:8.
2. Isa. 8:6, 7. Author's translation.
3. Zech. 7:2. The Hebrew states they were sent to the priests *at* Bayth-El (see NKJV margin and others). Zechariah was in Yerushalem, or Bayth-El.

enthusiasm recently for the completion of the house. They seemed more interested in continuing the pity party of the last seventy years than in getting the Bayth-El finished. I had to tell them from Yahweh that *He* is very jealous for Tzion and desires to dwell in the midst of Yerushalem. And He insisted I tell them it's the city of truth, His mountain, the holy mountain!—and oh, there was so much more, and that Yahweh expects the feasts to be joyful and truthful occasions that attract people from far and wide, and that just as *He* had to determine in the past to deprive us because of our provocation, He has now determined to do us good. Praised be the everlasting Yahweh!

    In my heart are the things to come, for in speaking of Yeshua, whom we have here and now crowned High Priest with a kingly crown, *He* has spoken through my lips of the One! He, Yeshua the Priest, is, I think, a shadow of Mashiach! I can—what is the word I seek?—I can taste His coming! Come quickly, Mashiach!

14

Ground Zero

> And they brought Him to *the place*.
> —Mark 15:22
> (NKJV, Grk. *ho topon* ; *emphasis added*)

> *He* shall bruise your head
> —Genesis 3:15b (NKJV)

It was dark—portently dark—and had been since midday. Scarlet rivulets caressed a small pyramid of cold stones. The pyramid served as additional support to a large timber stake standing out of a hole in rough ground. There had been an unusual amount of blood for a crucifixion, as it was not usual to pierce the victim. The rivulets on stone and dust, though red, shone now silver, now gold as they caught the dancing light of Roman torches. In the gloom of the three-hour darkness, this made the stake, and the tortured human form upon it appear to be supported by those shining rivulets as some ficus trees appear to stand on a pyramid of roots. In addition, quivering meniscus pools forming at the ends of the rivulets momentarily provided quicksilver bases in which they, in turn, took root. With little imagination, an observer could suppose that the rivulets actually flowed upward from their bases to support the form above. Viewed in this way, it could be a picture of history, of a culmination. For what had defined human history more, or more articulately, than blood?

Here was the culmination, the apex, and, more appropriately, the very crux of history's red tide; the event to which all other bloodshed, in one way or another, pointed. The stream, or streams, did in fact flow, both up to and down from the One called Son of Man, now nailed in extremis. For all but one of the soldiers who effected the grisly task, there was little recognition of this moment's moment. That one saw it and cried, in a cataclysm of regret, "Certainly this was the Son of God." His eyes, not as calloused as those of his colleagues, glimpsed, in a moment of epiphany, the enormity, almost beyond expression, of the travesty to which he had so recently put his hand.

Few observers of this dark and savage event could be analytical while they observed. The accompanying noises, images, and smells of crucifixion were overloading,

THE PLACE

sickening—salivating and barking dogs; the cries and moans of the anguished dying and bereaved living indistinguishable; the indifferent brutality of soldiers; the swirling, intermingling smells of vinegar and hyssop, sweat, urine, and body wastes; of torch oil burning and, in this particular case, the sight and sound of soldiers gaming for the coveted robe of one of the victims.

But after the event—well after—when the enormity and the weight of implications had trickled through the consciousness, when the immediacy of pain had diffused, a thinking observer might move to analysis. The picture etched now on stones of memory may begin to take on life and meaning. In the silver, mercuric streams now retrieved, he might begin to see the stream of human history; to imagine that all events prior to this grisly event somehow inevitably flowed to it, and that all things thereafter would flow from it. That this event indeed stood as the crux and locus of human history.

And it occurred at the place. Indeed, the record says (whether by design or strange coincidence, let the reader judge), "And they brought Him to the place, Golgotha which is translated Place of a Skull."[1] How like the Romans to make a mockery of the Temple by conducting crucifixion right there before it. The place is, therefore, indeed, the locus of human history and the only place at which and

---

1. Mark 15:22 NKJV

from which meaning can be derived. Without the place, we are left to invent hypotheses and systems that never answer the hollowness but merely contribute another layer to it. And so, according to this writer's understanding, the place where One called Eschatos Adam cried with a loud voice, "It is finished!" is exactly the place where the one, "Protos Adam," was drawn from the red dust of Palestine and where the one who failed in his mission is superseded by the One who succeeds. It is here at the locus, where all is brought together, where failure is redeemed, where death becomes life, and finally, where communion is restored, and Eschatos Adam sends His Spirit to Protos Adam to join us together. And of that event, I will let Petros speak, in a moment.

But there is something else here. For on that day for the ages, when *He* was killed, at the place, the "tree" on which He was stretched became the new tree of life. Behold, where once stood that tree that held so much promise for Adam now stood another, holding new promise of new life for all mankind. For Protos Adam, a prohibition prevented access to the first tree.

It had been a long, long journey for all his offspring to this day when a new tree was planted, providing free and open access for all! Access to the first tree and its fruit had been closed through the flesh of Protos Adam; access to the second was opened through the flesh of Eschatos Adam. And all who eat of the fruit of this Tree live, and not only live, but pass from the hollowness into the fullness.

15

I Am Petros

Come, to the Bayth-El of Yaakov...for out of Tzion shall go forth Torah, and the word of the Lord from Yerushalem.

—Isaiah 2:3 and Micah 4:2
(Author's paraphrase with Scripture4All Hebrew Interlinear Bible)

And it shall come to pass in *the place* where it was said to them (the Gentiles), "You are not my people." There they shall be called sons of the living God.

—Romans 9:26
(nkjv, parenthesis and emphasis added)

When *He* came in power on that extraordinary day of visitation of which Yoel had spoken, I, along with more than one hundred others, knew *Him* as we had never known Him, even though we had seen Him and been with Him in person! For suddenly *He* was within in a way that seemed more "within" than even our own selves! There came a subsuming of ourselves, of our own "I am," somehow with *His* "I Am," yet without any theft. Indeed, speaking for myself, I became more myself than ever I had been. It was a mystery, yet it was what *He* had told us to expect; and certainly, although we had some trepidation, we were in a place of expectancy. Indeed, we were in the place that throughout time had been strangely touched by Him! Still in our ears and certainly in our hearts were those last words instructing us not to depart from Hierousalem, but to wait for the promise of the Father, and that within "not many days," we would be *baptized*, if you please, in Holy Spirit. I can tell you that no one wanted to miss this, for we were all familiar with the prophets and with Dabid, and so, with the feast approaching, there was a tangible sense that *He* was close by. We had been prayerfully watching and waiting because in our hearts, which were strangely in accord, we all wanted to cooperate with whatever His plan might be!

To say that the day exceeded our expectation would be an understatement, for when *He* came, it was no subdued arrival! He made certain there was no mistaking the fulfillment. I am almost at a loss to describe it to you, but our dear brother Lucas, in his usual well-researched and detailed manner, has, although he was not present, given

THE PLACE

you a splendid account. He meticulously interviewed me and many others and has recorded what I said that day; it flowed from me as though the fountains of my great deep had been untapped! There was such a sudden seeing and knowing and understanding of the stream of His purpose that it just had to come forth—and apparently it did!

What especially excited me and the thousands who then gathered that day—and I must say whom *He* had brought into Heirousalem for the feast—was what *He* showed me about Dabid, about how Theos raised up Christos as the Ultimate Heir to the throne of our beloved Dabid. And I suddenly saw that "the throne" had been transferred, together with the Heir, from an earthly location in Hierousalem to a new locus—at Theos's right hand above—and that it was from that throne that *He* has poured out the right and power of citizenship to any and all who will receive it! Citizenship, that is, of *His* kingdom! I saw from the words of Dabid himself that the throne of Dabid was and had been but a kind of shadowy symbol of what exists elsewhere. It was at that point that many had brought home to their hearts just who *He* is and what they had done to Him, and a spirit of repentance and faith became theirs. Oh, hallelujah! For what a day it was. *He* is indeed the One who speaks with His mouth and fulfils with His hand.

And by and by, we saw that *we* had become as it's said in our language, "Oikos tou Theou"— the house of God! And yes, it occurred at *the place* where Yaakov of old had said, "This is none other than Bayth-El," or as you say, "house of God"! The stone he set up was, as it were, to materialize one day much later, as a house of stone. But now, in our time and at the same place, *He* has started work on a New House, not made of stone but of flesh! Living Stones! Surely these are things understood only by the Spirit who came so wonderfully that day during Pentecost. Had *He* not said that He would live in us, and we had been full of wonder? Have *we* not become the place where His glory dwells and where He touches earth? Oh, now we understand though can scarce take it in. Oh, and just as *He* caused His fire to fall at the setting up of the tabernacle and at the consecration of Solomon's temple, it fell too, on that day on His new temple!

Of course, as time went by, I had opportunity to strengthen the saints in the gatherings among our people as well as among Gentiles. What a story on its own, that is; how *He* showed me that they too belong, especially now that the locus is no longer here, in the place, and yet *is* here! For I see that the place is now within, individually and collectively, all those who receive His Spirit. While "the throne" is above, *He* sends the Spirit of His kingship and government right into every heart that receives it, and they become the place in new form. As I have been writing to beloved ones in various dispersed places, the place is now within and among as *He* builds *us* into a new Bayth-El, a *pneumatikos oikos*, a spiritual house where the offerings are spiritual ones that please Him, like thanksgiving and worship and a clean heart and mind. I see it like this: remember how our prophet Esaias wrote about Him as the cornerstone being laid in Tzion? The Stone rejected by men, but chosen by God? *He* is that Cornerstone from which the entire new "Bayth-El" is growing and to which it is anchored, finding in Him its alignment and its integrity.

Why, our dear brother Paulos, with whom I once had the occasional struggle over his emphasis on Gentiles, sees the same thing. He has written that *the place* is no longer a material location. He saw that the way into the Holy Place has been opened by our new High Priest, and that *He* has now become High Priest over a new Bayth-El.[1]

Paulos wrote also in his letter to young Timotheos another most curious thing about this new Bayth-El when he spoke about behavior within the *oikos tou Theou*—"the house of God." We all remember how Iakob set up his pillar at the place and anointed it and said, "This is the Bayth-El and the gate of heaven." With the great learning of our brother Paulos in the ancient Scriptures, surely he was thinking of Iakob when he described us, the Bayth-El, as "the pillar and ground of the truth!"[2]

These things are indeed glorious but are seen by the Spirit when *He* comes to dwell in the place.

---

1. Heb. 10:21. Grk. (Anglicized) oikos tou theou, house of God.
2. 1 Tim. 3:15 NKJV

16

The Place Gets a Makeover!

The old man's face shone, reminding his visitors of what they had read of Moses after his Sinai encounter with *Him*. They felt they were in the presence of one who had been close to the Holy.

Eventually, a visitor spoke. It was Gaius. "Johannes, why is it that *He* has spoken so graphically through you of the things to come?"

In the half-light of dusk and just before the lamps were lit, the three visitors leaned forward expectantly, the better to both hear and see the man whose remarkable visions during incarceration on Patmos had brought them to his bedside. Gaius's question seemed to hang in the warm air before the old man answered.

"You have seen," he began, "all the pageantry and pomp and color and noise of Rome and how pervasive and, indeed, persuasive it is?" It was really a question, to which the two men and one woman nodded in response. They had indeed seen it; saw it every day as centurions and consuls and praetors and magistrates and tribunes, with all regalia and show, made the presence of emperor and empire real among the common people. The trumpets blew and standards and flags flew, reinforcing the triumphalism of Rome's government. And as well, there were the roads and buildings and infrastructure and commerce that all boasted success and efficacy.

The old man continued, "It is triumphal and messianic in its message, persuading many, but it is a lie. We are to be subject to it as the instrument of God for law and order, but when it pretends to be able to solve the problem of the heart of man, it lies. The clothing and the fanfare and the pomp and display, not to mention that it has overcome by sheer might many lesser nations – these all persuade many that a lasting salvation for all has arrived or is at least near."

"It will crumble?" asked the woman whose name was Julia and whose graying hair was adorned with a colorful scarf of purple. She smelled of lotions and perfume and had a soft, smiling, and pretty face. She was the wife of Gaius.

"Of course, as will all lies. They will eventually all be overcome and shown for what they are by the Truth. Indeed, a common theme and word through all that *He* has shown me is in that word of ours, *nikao*." (In the language of the reader, the meaning is "conquer, overcome, triumph.") "As

THE PLACE

we committed the visions to the parchments, there it was, again and again, something like fourteen times! The visions are about which city, which system, and which Lord finally prevails—and it is not Caesar or Rome!"

"Ah, so what *He* is saying is that even though human systems may look triumphant or messianic or may pretend to be able to overcome human problems, there is but one who truly overcomes? But one Messiah?" blurted out the other man, Demetrius.

"There you have it," says Johannes, pulling himself off the bed and into a standing position with the aid of his staff. "That is the entire message of the visions. What *He* showed me was splendor and pageantry and authority that far outweighs the shallow pretences of Rome. She may have her graphic...shall we say...in-your-face display, but it all hides a big lie."

The reason he had stood was to open a shutter in the western wall of the rooftop room and to point outward with his staff. As he opened the shutter the room immediately blazed with red-orange splendor. The view from the hillside dwelling in Ephesus was westward over several other dwellings and important buildings, and more distant, the Aegean Sea all gold and ashimmer as a huge liquid orange sun plunged into it.

"Come and look at this sight. Even my aging eyes never tire of it," said Johannes. He shook his bearded head in wonder. They joined him and stood for those lingering moments in awe as the sea grew purple, the cirrus clouds above swept brush strokes of lush crimson paint across a velvet sky, and a hush descended. It led him to say, "The glory of Rome also has blazed and will fade, just as did Greece and Persia, but praise the Lord, the kingdom to which we belong will never fade or die or diminish—and it rules over all and triumphs over all!" There was such certainty and assurance and rest in both his words and his voice that the others rejoiced at the inward knowing that seemed to be transmitted to them.

"But you said city. You said it's about which city prevails, did you not, dear brother Johannes?" The question came from the woman who looked perplexed. "Why a city? We've heard that your beloved Hierousalem is in uproar and under grave threat because temple silver has been plundered by the procurator to offset lost tax revenue. If Rome's anger is aroused, the city surely will not stand."

"Ah, my child," says the old man with a gesture that quickly has them all seated once more. "The city Hierousalem is but a shadow. It will fall, as our dear Lord told us, and it will have a rising again of a sort, but it's what it represents that is of importance now, for it represents something greater and something eternal. Why, our beloved brother Paulos has also written wonderfully of it to Hebrew believers." He shuffled some parchment rolls on a table at the side of his bed and, in doing so, almost started a fire as one brushed into a lamp newly lit by a sweet young

THE PLACE

aide who had silently come in with bread and water and cheese. Johannes quickly snuffed out the little flame on the parchment corner with his fingers and then said, "I had a copy of some of his words about this subject made. Listen to this." And he read, holding the skin at an angle to the lamplight and squinting to make out the letters.

> For you have not come to the mountain that may be touched and that burned with fire, and to blackness and darkness and tempest, and the sound of a trumpet and the voice of words so that those who heard it begged that the word should not be spoken to them anymore.
>
> But you have come to Mount Zion and to the city of the living God, the heavenly Heirousalem, to an innumerable company of angels, to the general assembly and church of the firstborn who are registered in heaven, to God the judge of all, to the spirits of just men made perfect.[1]

Johannes's face was alight with more than the lamplight. "That is just what *He* showed *me*! Paulos said that he was taken to the third heaven, so I believe he glimpsed it too! And I know that he wrote to others too about what he called the Heirousalem that is above.[2] You see, it seems

---

1. Heb. 12:18–23 NKJV excerpts.
2. See Gal. 4:25, 26.

that we, the redeemed, occupy the fulfillment of the place that has its shadow—just an echo really—in our earthly Heirousalem, complete with the stream that flows within it and from it. That's why I too called it *the place* in my account of our Lord's life and ministry.[3] I wanted everyone to know that where *He* died was just near the place that belonged to our beloved Heirousalem. Everyone had been calling it the place since antiquity. You only have to look at the writings of our fathers and the ones about the Maccabees[4] to know that, and that's what I've always called it too."

"You mean the temple and the spring at Gihon?" queried Timotheos.

"The same, and it reminds me so much of the words our Lord spoke that I set down in what I wrote about Him

---

3. See for example, John 11:48 "And the Romans will come and take away *the place* (of us) and the nation (of us)" author's translation emphasis added. John 19:19–20 Grk. *o topos*, see particularly Darby's Translation—and as the Greek actually reads, "This title therefore many of the Jews read, for *the place* of the city where Jesus was crucified, was near; and it was written in Hebrew, Greek, Latin." See also John 4:20 where the Samaritan woman says, "You Jews say that *in* Jerusalem is *the place* where one ought to worship." (NKJV, emphasis added) (Note: Not "Jerusalem is the place.")

4. See 2 Macc. 1:14; 2:18; 3:18; 5:16–17, and 10:7. For example, 2 Macc. 1:14 speaks about Antiochus's intention to marry the goddess: "On the pretext of marrying the goddess, Antiochus with his friends had come to *the place* (emphasis added) to get its great treasures as a dowry." The context reveals that the place is the temple.

some time ago. It's as though I can hear Him saying them now! It was on the last great day of our great Feast of the Tabernacles when the water from Gihon is poured, and we were there in the temple courts." Johannes was becoming breathless and had to pause a moment, then he continued. "Yes, Yesous our Lord cried out so loudly that everyone heard—it was amazing—'He who believes in Me...out of his heart will flow rivers of living water.'"[5]

"So believers become just like the temple and Gihon? With the *living* water springing up in them and flowing from them?" It was Julia this time, caught up in the symbolic elegance of it all.

But then Johannes had more to say. "Now you have it, and so many have seen this 'living water.' It's a favorite picture from our Father. You'll remember that Iezekiel and Zacharias and Joel too saw it flowing from the temple throne room where *He* dwelled between the cherubim. And, of course, in the songs of our Lord's great father Dabid, the Korahites sing of Tzion: "His foundation is in the holy mountains...and all my springs are in You" and "the Lord sits enthroned over the flood."[6] Yes, that bubbling spring beneath the throne is a humble picture from the natural world of what *He* has made to exist in the spiritual world.

---

5   John 7:38 NKJV
6   Ps. 87 and Ps. 29:10.

He gave it to us so that when *He* speaks about spiritual things, we already have a picture in our minds."

And suddenly Julia, prompted by what Johannes had quoted from Dabid, burst forth, interrupting Johannes midsentence. "Of course, of course, for in the Psalm about God being our refuge, does it not say, 'There is a river whose streams make glad the city of God, the holy place of the tabernacle of Most High...The Lord of Hosts is with us and the *God of Yiacob* is our refuge?'[7] It's one of my favorites, and yet I've only just seen the significance of the stream at the holy place!" Julia could scarcely contain the excitement of the revelation.

"Yes, yes, for I saw a river, clear as crystal, proceeding from the throne where *He* sat. Yes, just as Gihon has sprung up and flowed right beneath the golden ark in our temple at Heirousalem all these years. It is a shadow. It is an echo and a symbol of that which exists in *His* realm—something that is as far greater than your shadow on that wall as you are."

The stoop that characterized the old man Johannes suddenly and momentarily seemed to vanish as he saw in his memory that which he had seen in his extraordinary visions. Once more he stood erect, eyes fixed on the wall opposite and on the shadow of Gaius as he retold the vivid detail.

---

7. Psalms 46:4, 7, author's translation; emphasis added.

"I've never seen the temple." Gaius too was now mesmerized by both the words and his shadow. "I had plans to travel to Heirousalem before I heard of what is now taking place. It will surely be destroyed. How sad it all is, and I'm sure it is another reason why *He* has given you these wonderful visions to share with us all—Oh, how good is our Lord!"

Johannes went on. "You know, there is a good description written by one Flavius Josephus, a historian and a Jew, although as far as I know, not a follower of our Lord. I have seen copies of his writings in the library even here in Ephesus, so perhaps you could ask to see them. Although he doesn't seem to speak directly of the spring, he quotes Hecateus, who describes the temple in the middle of the city when viewed from the east from *Oros Ton Elaiōn* (Mount of Olives).[8] Other eyewitnesses such as Tacitus and even an Egyptian, Aristeas, describe the actual spring

---

8. Josephus: Contra Apion I.22. Hecataeus of Abdera, quoted by Josephus.

within the temple!"⁹ Johannes reflected momentarily before continuing with a new thought. "You know," he said with a tone of discovery. "How appropriate that a spring of life-giving water has been so central...so germane to *His* plan and the long history of thirstiness since the loss at the very beginning."

"And the city? Tell us about the city," reminded Julia.

"Ah yes, like nothing earthly, nothing temporal. Something from *His* world coming to a new earth. Not comprehensible but glorious and inhabited by all who've loved Him, but now made new as spirit beings. And with everything once intended, restored, the river, the tree of life, and *He* Himself as the temple in the midst, oh, it was as real as this room yet oh so different. It was what was real, and all this"—he waved his staff around the room and pointed it outside as well—"all this, suddenly shadowy! Dim and becoming dimmer, a mere and poor reflection and idea of the real! But it's the city that overcame. For I saw its

---

9. Letter of eyewitness Aristeas (around 285 bc, 83--91): "The whole of the floor is paved with stones and slopes down to the appointed places, that water may be conveyed to wash away the blood from the sacrifices, for many thousand beasts are sacrificed there on the feast days. And there is an inexhaustible supply of water, because an abundant natural spring gushes up from within the temple area. There are moreover wonderful and indescribable cisterns underground , they pointed out to me, at a distance of five furlongs all round the site of the temple, and each of them has countless pipes so that the different streams converge together."

counterpart, Babylon, as a harlot, and her champion a great and ugly monster. But this *New Heirousalem*, why, it left Babylon for dead in splendor and integrity and rightness, and its Champion and Mascot was...the Lamb, who was slain since the foundation."

The three sat spellbound because Johannes painted such colorful word pictures. It was clear that he had experienced a special prison visitation from the One who had said, "*I* was in prison, and *you* visited *Me*"!

As he spoke, they could see the great overcoming city descending to occupy a new earth and banishing all other pretences and lies that men had tried to build for their own salvation.

As they three took their leave from the now-infirm Johannes, they talked among themselves excitedly as they made their way back to lodgings in the city.

Gaius said, "Now I see the importance of the imagery."

"Me too," said Demetrius. "And how special is the idea of the spring. I'm sure the believers who live in Heirousalem must have seen it more clearly than us. How blessed we have been to have Johannes explain it more fully. That stream, that spring, at the very place where Iacob said so long ago, "This is the Bayth-El. This is *oikos tou Theou*! What a beautiful picture of *His* work and plan for us."

Julia, who had been walking silently beside her husband, now spoke. "Since I've known the Lord, I've had that profound sense that this world is really but a shadow, ephemeral and transient. My heart knows that the real world is that which *He* inhabits and which lasts forever. We are inclined to make so much of this material and transitory place, but Johannes already lives more in the other place than this. He already breathes its air and has little attachment to what we see about us, even though he greatly admires its beauty."

"Just being with him helps change my perspective," chimed in Gaius again. "Gives you a sense of proportion, challenges me to spend more time with *Him* from whom the right perspective comes! And Johannes is so right about the imagery and presence of Rome being so persuasive. I have to confess there are times when it's easy to start looking in that direction with my needs, even though I know better. It certainly does hold out a kind of messianic prospect. But we know and thank God that as we have experienced—there is only one Messiah."

"Hallelujah!" cried Demetrius, not usually given to such expletive.

And so they all said, "Hallelujah, praise the Lord God Almighty."

And so they talked and walked and walked and talked, exhausting their wonder at the idea of the ages; the idea that *He* has always had in mind an abode for Himself; the idea that a physical Hierusalem here was but a shadowy hint of the place He really has in mind; the grand idea of us becoming one with Him in the greatest marriage ever consummated and also becoming the city and dwelling in which *He* takes up virtual residence for whatever He plans for ages eternal. And so they speculated and rejoiced and expended themselves until they were brought back to earth by arrival at their humble lodgings and parted for the evening with thanksgiving to their Lord for the opportunity to be with one who walked so close to his Master.

Appendix 1

Here are further clues from the New Testament and other writings that reinforce the view that the temple in the time of Jesus was in the center of the City of David and above Gihon Spring:

On several occasions, the Gospel writers mention Jesus leaving the temple and going out to the Mount of Olives, and returning from there to the temple.

On these occasions, He was residing (or possibly sleeping out) somewhere on the Mount of Olives. More than likely, He would have been at the house of a disciple or supporter, overnight. It is clear that He resided on some occasions at Bethany (which was probably on the easterly slopes of the Mount of Olives) at the home of Lazarus and Martha. Most authorities believe Bethany was about a mile (1.6 kilometers) from Jerusalem.

There was a period where Jesus was back and forth to the temple *daily* (see John 7:53–8:2, Luke 21:37–38 and 22:39) which discloses that during this period, He was teaching *daily* in the temple. Both John and Luke inform us that He would arrive at daybreak (Grk. *orthros*, John 8:2) and that the people arrived at daybreak to hear His teaching (Luke 21:38), and His custom was to retreat to Olives at the end of the day (Luke 22:39 "as was His custom," Grk. *ethos*, "habit or institution").

Now at least one of these occasions (and almost certainly more) was a Sabbath (see Luke 22:7 and Matt. 26:17, "the Day of Unleavened Bread") and as the maximum permitted journey on Sabbath was two thousand cubits, or about nine hundred meters, we have to assume that He had chosen the residence or place in which He stayed due both to its proximity and ease of access to the temple, and also so as not to create unnecessary offense to disciples or others conscious of Sabbath observance.

As there was no accusation leveled at Jesus by the Pharisees who were watching every move, and even picked Him up over disciples gleaning some barley to eat on Sabbath (Luke 6:1–5 and Matt. 12:1–8), we can safely assume that His "digs" were within the prescribed Sabbath limits, that is, within sight of the temple just across Kidron to His west.

That this was so is made even clearer by Luke in Acts 1 just prior to and after Jesus's ascension. Jesus had been speaking with the disciples and spending time with them for forty days, and it is clear from verse 4 that just prior to His ascension, they were assembled with Him. That assembly was pretty certain to be at the place where He was *accustomed* to go, as we've discussed above. Luke, a most meticulous researcher and writer, tells us that after Jesus's ascension, the disciples "returned to Jerusalem *from* the mount called Olivet, which is *near* Jerusalem, *a Sabbath day's* journey" (Acts 1:12, NKJV, emphasis added), so within about nine hundred meters. Of further interest is that Luke here, as in his Gospel (Luke 21:37) calls the area from which they returned Olivet. This seems to refer to the southern tip or end and slopes of the ridge that forms the entire Mount of Olives.

In Mark's account of the days around final Passover (14:12–26), the man to whom the disciples were directed and in whose house in Jerusalem Jesus would institute His new covenant "feast" would be carrying a pitcher of water, an unusual duty for a man and therefore noticeable. According to Luke's account, they would encounter Him "upon entering the city," and therefore it seems a reasonable assumption that the gate the two disciples used for entry was the Fountain Gate at Gihon, where the man had collected water and which they were accustomed to use with Jesus as they went back and forth between their "digs" and the temple during those final days of His ministry.

A further reference of interest is that in Mark 13:1–4, where again Jesus was leaving the temple and the disciples commented about the impressive stones. Jesus prophetically declared that "not one stone will be left upon another that shall not be thrown down" (which, by the way, if taken literally and fulfilled literally, means that the western wall is not what it is held to be!).

Once again, Jesus headed to Olives, as by custom, where He sat, wrote Mark, "opposite the temple" (Grk. *katenanti* means "opposite, *in front of*") while His disciples question Him about when this will occur. It appears that His accomodation was on the western slope of Olives, just opposite and in close view of the temple, where they could easily see the great stones of which they were speaking.

Now in case it's argued that this could still mean that the temple was in the traditionally held position, the problems are as follows:

The temple at the traditional site would have been at an elevation of about 740 meters. If the temple was there, to attain the same elevation or higher for any reasonable view of it from Olives across Kidron to the east would require a lateral distance of about five hundred meters—especially as it was supposedly set back somewhat from the bluff that forms the edge of the slope down to Kidron. Second, it would almost certainly put the residence in which Jesus stayed beyond the limit of a Sabbath day's journey as the walk down into Kidron and up the other side would exceed that.

However, if as I posit, the temple was sited above Gihon Spring in the middle of the rough crescent that defined the City of David, its elevation would be considerably lower by some fifty meters—about 690 meters. At that point,

THE PLACE

Kidron is narrow and steep, and the lateral distance across at the 690-meter elevation is only about 200 or perhaps 250 meters. When at the same level as the temple but on the opposite side of Kidron, Jesus and His associates would have felt as though they could reach out and touch it! The accompanying contour map makes this clear.

A further convincing clue is disclosed by Luke, writing about Paul in Jerusalem in Acts chapter 21. The commotion caused by Paul's teaching at the temple aroused the whole city and soon came to the attention of the military authorities. Having been dragged from the temple by the Jews, who then closed the temple gates, news reached the Commander of the Roman troops stationed in Jerusalem. His and their station, as we know from other sources, was the Fortress of Antonia[10], which, if the traditional siting of the temple on (so-called) Temple Mount was correct, would place it somewhere *lower* down the hill from the temple. But this cannot be so because Luke tells us (v.32) that the soldiers ran *down* to the crowd at the temple. We must conclude that the fortress was higher in elevation than, the temple!

---

10 Built by Herod the Great around 19 BC and named after his patron Mark Antony.

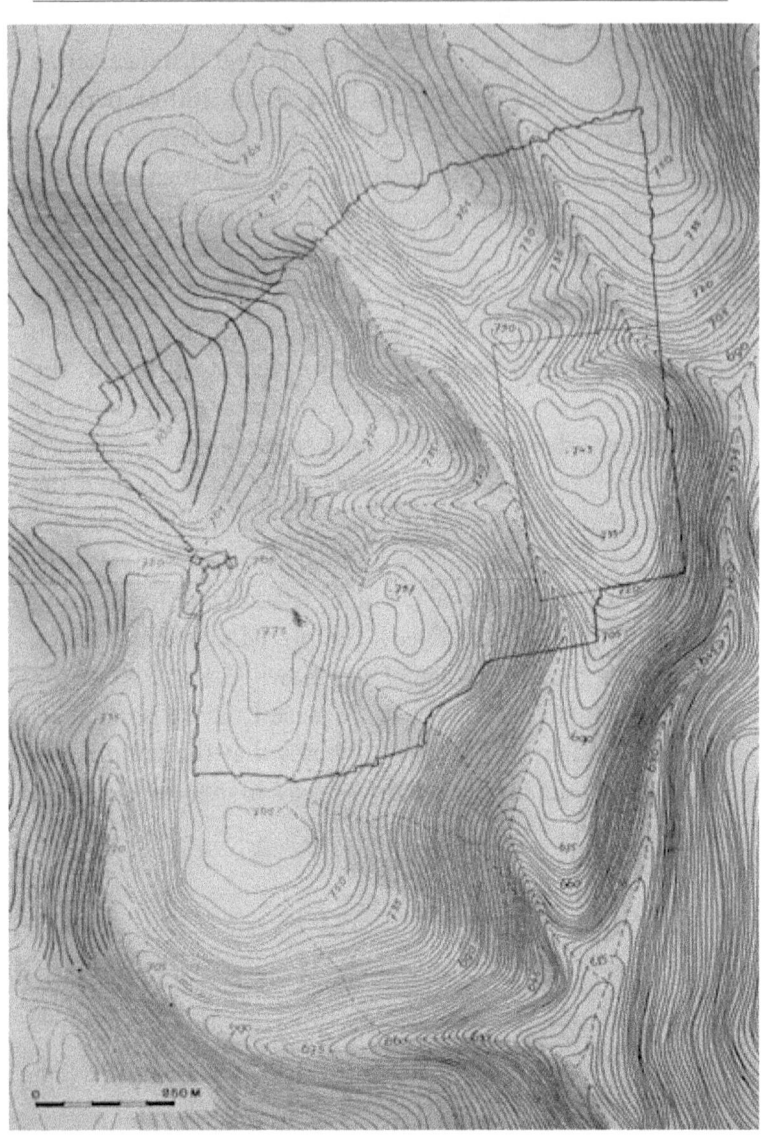

www.ingramcontent.com/pod-product-compliance
Lightning Source LLC
Chambersburg PA
CBHW071504150426
43191CB00009B/1412